D1163276

8

THE PRAISE OF LINCOLN

THE
PRAISE OF LINCOLN

AN ANTHOLOGY

COLLECTED AND ARRANGED BY

A. DALLAS WILLIAMS

INDIANAPOLIS
THE BOBBS-MERRILL COMPANY
PUBLISHERS

Acknowledgment

The editor of this Anthology desires to express his sincere thanks to many publishers and authors for their courtesy in granting permission to use selections from their various volumes. His thanks are due the following publishers: The Houghton Mifflin Company, Boston, for the use of poems by Thomas Bailey Aldrich, Edmund Clarence Stedman, Bayard Taylor, Richard Watson Gilder, James Russell Lowell, Alice Cary, Phœbe Cary, Christopher Pearce Cranch, Lucy Larcom, Oliver Wendell Holmes, John Greenleaf Whittier, John Townsend Trowbridge, Edna Dean Proctor, Julia Ward Howe, Rose Terry Cooke, Edward Rowland Sill, Jones Very, Wendell Phillips Garrison, Maurice Thompson, John Vance Cheney, Nora Perry, Henry Howard Brownell; The Macmillan company, New York, the poem by Percy Mackaye; D. Appleton and Company, New York, for the use of poems by William Cullen Bryant; The Saalfield Publishing Company, Akron, Ohio, poem by Phœbe A. Hanaford; Silver Burdett and Company, New York, poem by Samuel Francis Smith; Longmans, Green and Company, New York, poems by John James Piatt; The J. B. Lippincott Company, Philadelphia, poem by George Henry Boker; G. P. Putnam's Sons, New York, poems from *Abraham Lincoln,* by Lyman Whitney Allen, and from *Survivals,* by Lewis V. Randolph; The Funk and Wagnalls Company, New York, poem by Richard Realf; David McKay, Philadelphia, poems by Walt Whitman; Charles Scribner's Sons, New York, poems by Richard

ACKNOWLEDGMENT

Henry Stoddard; The New England Publishing Company, Boston, poem by Hezekiah Butterworth; The Lothrop, Lee and Shepard Company, Boston, poem by Robert Henry Newell; Thomas Y. Crowell and Company, New York, poem by Frank B. Sanborn; Little, Brown and Company, Boston, poem by Edith Colby Banfield; Harper and Brothers, New York, poem by Herman Melville, from his *Battle Pieces and Aspects of the War*, and poems from *The Poetical Works of Charles Graham Halpine*.

Acknowledgments are due the following periodicals and magazines for permission to include poems that appeared originally in their pages: The American Magazine, The Independent, Youth's Companion, The Atlantic Monthly, Success Magazine, Hampton's Magazine and The Century.

Thanks are also due the American Press Association, for permission to use *An Appreciation of Lincoln*, by Robertus Love.

The authors named below have graciously added their consent to that of their publishers: John E. Barrett, Virginia Frazer Boyle, Edna Dean Proctor, Robertus Love, Julia Ward Howe, Phœbe A. Hanaford, Joel Benton, Eugene J. Hall, Lyman Whitney Allen, Robert Mackay, Horace Spencer Fiske, James Nicoll Johnston, William Henry Venable, Percy Mackaye, John Townsend Trowbridge, Florence Evelyn Pratt, Margaret E. Sangster, Edwin Markham, James Oppenheim, Frank B. Sanborn, John Vance Cheney, Samuel E. Kiser, William Wilberforce Newton, the Reverend Doctor P. C. Croll, Wilbur D. Nesbit, the Reverend Levi Lewis Hager, Lewis V. F.

ACKNOWLEDGMENT

Randolph, Doctor S. Weir Mitchell, Benjamin S. Parker, General John James Piatt, Nathan Haskell Dole, and Laura Redden Searing; while Mr. and Mrs. P. McK. Garrison have given permission to include the poem by their father, Wendell Phillips Garrison.

By special arrangement with Edward William Thomson we include in the volume his poems entitled: *We Talked of Lincoln, When Lincoln Died,* and *Father Abraham Lincoln,* from his volume *When Lincoln Died and other Poems,* published by the Houghton Mifflin Company, Boston.

A. D. W.

INTRODUCTION

The poetic faculty is the one divine gift which has no limitations in time or space. It sings in every note of love, from passion to sacrifice. It tunes its lyre to the primrose pitch; and its music is heard in the diapason of the spheres. It records with equal fervor the glories of war and the beauties of peace, the white man's burden and the black man's care, the thrill of liberty and the sullen silence of the slave, the peace of home and the pleasures of the harem, the pomp of power and the pride of place. It weaves Jacob's coat of poverty and Solomon's royal robe. It paints with equal touch the passion of a Madonna and a Salome. It carries to Paradise the warrior's cry, the lover's sigh and the penitential tear. With love and patriotism it forms the human trinity. It ascends to heaven, and, Lucifer-like, drops swiftly to hell again. It has flattered Nero on his throne and consoled Milton in his blindness. It has cajoled, caressed, rebuked, uplifted, dismayed mankind. It dispenses the honey of Hymettus and the poison of asps. It has recorded the agony of Mary and the anguish of Cleopatra. It is good and evil, bitterness and sweetness, light and darkness, help and hindrance. From its mouth have come both blessings and cursings. Happy the man who is worthy of its glorifications.

America stands for something or for nothing. I am one of those who believe it stands for something. It is the one land where the mystery of manhood may be fully revealed; where, at the last, not race nor creed nor station, but character shall win and purposes shall be the weights put in the balances of judgment. It is the land of hope and not despair. If I were asked to tell why thus I think, I should say that what has been may be. If I were called upon to name one man who proved my statement I should answer, Abraham Lincoln. And with the name all doubt would vanish and the babel of discordant views become dumb. Before you would arise his tall, majestic figure, sharply silhouetted against a nineteenth century sky, and you would see passing before you the years wherein he walked from the Nation's poverty to the Nation's Pantheon. He proved our country's right to be, and our power to be right. Who walks in his steps in public or in private life will always be enrolled in the Army of Constitutional Liberty. His is the one life in our history we can not too often review nor too sedulously emulate. We may forget all others, but while we remember him in the true sense of remembrance we shall be safe. Too much can not be said or sung of him. He can not too often be recalled to the memory of this people. The marble and the bronze are enriched by his homely face. The pigment takes on a richer color as it traces his counterfeit presentment. And when the poet sweeps his strings in music to the greatness and the goodness of this typical American, his chords approach the divine—for it was given Lincoln to die for a people.

Anthologies are not new. But to gather the roses which have bloomed from the life of our greatest man and from his memory, and to let the American people behold their beauty and enjoy their perfume is a distinct feature in American literature. May this vol-

INTRODUCTION

ume be read; and as we read it may we vow that this government "of the people, by the people, for the people, shall not perish from the earth."

Thos. R. Marshall

April 11th, 1911.

Lincoln's Literary Taste

A remarkable group of human beings had drifted from many points to the top of Salem Hill in Illinois, and were living there in small log cabins from '30 to '38. It was an eminence commanding an extensive view of broad, green prairies, cut by the winding Sangamon which touched the foot of the hill. In one of the cabins lived Doctor John Allen, a graduate of Dartmouth and a man of character and cultivation, who had gone west seeking a climate favorable to weak lungs. Another little log cabin was the home of one Jack Kelso, of whom little is known save that he was fond of the flowing jug and spent his days fishing in the river or shooting on the near prairies, where game was abundant. It is probable that he was the dissolute son of a family in the East able to give him an allowance and perhaps glad to be relieved of his proximity. It is known that he was a man of some taste in letters and familiar with the poetry of Burns and Shakespeare, often quoted in his conversation. The schoolmaster, Mentor Graham, a man of considerable learning and probably a college graduate, also lived on Salem Hill. These three men represented the culture of the East.

There was also in the little settlement a preacher

of the name of Cameron, who is said to have been a man of parts. Of him, however, little is known.

The Rutledges from Kentucky, who kept the mill and the log inn were, I take it, simple back-country folk of excellent character. James Rutledge would seem to have been a "well-posted man" to use a phrase of the time, of sound opinions on religion and politics.

Such was the aristocracy of Salem Hill when Lincoln came there in his young manhood. The other settlers were mostly the moving riff-raff of a pioneer time from here and there—quaint, restless, unrooted folk seeking an easy fortune and never finding it. The young giant was himself a restless mover, his spirit seeking its way, when his boat stuck on the dam at New Salem on the Sangamon. The beauty of the high hill and its commanding view no doubt appealed to him. It is beyond a doubt, also, that his personality appealed to the lonely dwellers on the hilltop. I try to imagine how they would have gathered about him at Rutledge's tavern that evening and listened to his droll talk. I am sure that he would have enjoyed telling them of his adventures on the river and that they would have enjoyed the story.

I can hear the laughter as I think of it. How Doctor Allen and Jack Kelso and James Rutledge and Mentor Graham would have warmed to the honest-hearted, humorous young stranger within their gates! They would have given him a hearing the like of which he had never known. He would have heard, and probably for the first time in his life, the captivating rhythm of Burns—how the wisdom it carried would have delighted him!—and the noble music of Shakespeare. Allen's dignity would have captured the young prophet of the back woods who, I presume, had never enjoyed intimate talk with a real gentleman.

Then the eyes of pretty Ann Rutledge would have been among those which were looking at the young giant that evening.

He liked these people and they liked him, and he decided to be one of them. Long before that day he had acquired an indefinite ambition and the love of honor and human decency. There he was to get a love for literature and a longing to serve. He began to study grammar and a musty old volume of Blackstone which he had rooted out of a barrel. The abundant leisure which he enjoyed in the little log store of Berry & Lincoln was favorable to his purpose. Every day he was getting poorer, but he was also getting wiser.

The immediate background of his growing literary genius would seem to be three great passions. Two of them came to him on Salem Hill—a deep patriotism and the love of Ann Rutledge. The other passion was inborn. It was the love of his fellow men, coupled with an understanding of them which no one in the range of my knowledge has shown. These three *things are as the ink of his pen until 1863, when a new element imparts to his work an immortal rhythm—a deep religious feeling born of the great trials through which he had passed.*

The late Horace White has rightly written: "One got the overwhelming conviction that Lincoln was charged with an irresistible and inspiring sense of duty to his fellow men."

The first fruit of the little school of New Salem life was a crude speech delivered in 1838, full of patriotic fervor and fairly well phrased, but lacking in restraint. Not until twenty years later had he "found his center," as Henry M. Alden used to put it, and become familiar with his range of mastery and content to keep within it. Then he delivered the famous lost speech, written on the backs of envelopes and scraps of paper, of which all that remains is its tremendous effect and certain phrases like: "A house divided against itself must fall."

One of the most curious examples of his literary art was that which caused the wrath of his enemies to praise him.

Judge Douglas had publicly denounced Lincoln and declared his intention of chastising him.

Lincoln's answer, full of good nature, was as follows:

"In the first place a fight would prove nothing at issue in this election. It might prove that the Judge

was a more muscular man than I or that I am stronger than he, but this subject is not referred to in either of the platforms. My second reason for declining such an encounter with Judge Douglas is that he doesn't want it himself. He and I are about the best friends in the world and when we get together he would no more think of fighting me than he would think of fighting his wife. Therefore when he spoke of fighting he was not giving vent to ill feeling but only trying to excite—well, let us say, enthusiasm against me in this audience."

This surely is a pretty bit of literary art.

Below are examples of his forming style. The lucid and forceful manner that Lincoln had attained by 1857 is well shown in the following terse reply to an argument then widely current:

"Now I protest against the counterfeit logic which concludes that because I do not want a black woman for a slave I must necessarily want her for a wife. I need not have her for either. I can just leave her alone. In some respects she certainly is not my equal; but in her natural right to eat the bread she earns with her own hands without asking leave of any one else, she is my equal, and the equal of all others."

How often he utters words that seem prophetic. As early as 1856 he had declared in his best argumentative style:

"Do you say that such restriction of slavery would

be unconstitutional, and that some of the States would not submit to its enforcement? . . . The Supreme Court of the United States is the tribunal to decide such a question, and we will submit to its decisions; and if you do also there will be an end of the matter. Will you? If not, who are the disunionists—you or we? We, the majority, would not strive to dissolve the Union; and if any attempt is made, it must be by you, who so loudly stigmatize us as disunionists. But the Union, in any event, will not be dissolved."

Undoubtedly William H. Seward, a man of exquisite literary taste, had been a help to Lincoln in mounting to the lonely summit of style which he attained in the speech at Gettysburg and the second inaugural.

IRVING BACHELLER.

THE PRAISE OF LINCOLN

O CAPTAIN! MY CAPTAIN!

Walt Whitman

O CAPTAIN! my Captain! our fearful trip is done,
The ship has weathered every wrack, the prize we
      sought is won,
The port is near, the bells I hear, the people all exulting,
While follow eyes the steady keel, the vessel grim and
      daring;

        But O heart! heart! heart!
          O the bleeding drops of red,
        Where on the deck my Captain lies,
          Fallen cold and dead!

O Captain! my Captain! rise up and hear the bells;
Rise up—for you the flag is flung—for you the bugle
      trills,
For you bouquets and ribboned wreaths—for you the
      shores a-crowding,
For you they call, the swaying mass, their eager faces
      turning.

        Here Captain! dear father!
          This arm beneath your head!
        It is some dream that on the deck
          You've fallen cold and dead.

I

THE PRAISE OF LINCOLN

My Captain does not answer, his lips are pale and still;
My father does not feel my arm, he has no pulse nor
    will;
The ship is anchored safe and sound, its voyage closed
    and done,
From fearful trip the victor ship comes in with object
    won.

    Exult, O shores, and ring, O bells!
      But I with mournful tread,
    Walk the deck my Captain lies
      Fallen cold and dead.

THE DEATH OF LINCOLN

William Cullen Bryant

OH, slow to smite and swift to spare,
    Gentle and merciful and just!
Who, in the fear of God didst bear
    The sword of power, a nation's trust.

In sorrow by thy bier we stand,
    Amid the awe that hushes all,
And speak the anguish of a land
    That shook with horror at thy fall.

Thy task is done; the bond are free;
    We bear thee to an honored grave,
Whose proudest monument shall be
    The broken fetters of a slave.

Pure was thy life; its bloody close
    Hath placed thee with the sons of light,
Among the noblest host of those
    Who perished in the cause of right.

2

HYMN TO ABRAHAM LINCOLN

William Wilberforce Newton

I

SAW you in his boyhood days
  O'er Kentucky's prairies;
Bending to the settler's ways
Yon poor youth whom now we praise,—
  Romance like the fairies?
Hero! Hero! Sent from God!
  Leader of his people.

II

Saw you in the days of youth
  By the candle's flaring:
Lincoln searching for the truth,
Splitting rails to gain, forsooth,
  Knowledge for the daring?
Hero! Hero! Sent from God!
  Leader of his people.

III

Saw you in his manhood's prime
  Like a star resplendent:
Him we praise in measured rhyme
Waiting for the coming time
  With a faith transcendent?
Hero! Hero! Sent from God!
  Leader of his people.

IV

Saw you in the hour of strife
  When fierce war was raging;
Him who gave the slaves a life

3

Full and rich with freedom rife,
  All his powers engaging?
Hero! Hero! Sent from God!
  Leader of his people.

V

Saw you when the war was done
  (Such is Lincoln's story)
Him whose strength the strife had won
Sinking like the setting sun
  Crowned with human glory?
Hero! Hero! Sent from God!
  Leader of his people.

VI

Saw you in our country's roll
  Midst her saints and sages:
Lincoln's name upon the scroll—
Standing at the topmost goal
  On the nation's pages?
Hero! Hero! Sent from God!
  Leader of his people.

VII

Hero! Yes! We know thy fame;
  It will live for ever!
Thou to us art still the same;
Great the glory of thy name,
  Great thy strong endeavor!
Hero! Hero! Sent from God!
  Leader of his people.

FROM
THE "COMMEMORATION ODE"

James Russell Lowell

LIFE may be given in many ways,
And loyalty to truth be sealed
As bravely in the closet as the field,
So bountiful is Fate;
But then to stand beside her,
When craven churls deride her,
To front a lie in arms and not to yield,
This shows, methinks, God's plan
And measure of a stalwart man,
Limbed like the old heroic breeds,
Who stands self-poised on manhood's solid earth,
Not forced to frame excuses for his birth,
Fed from within, with all the strength he needs.

Such was he, our martyr chief,
Whom late the nation he had led
With ashes on her head,
Wept with the passion of an angry grief;
Forgive me if from present things I turn
To speak what in my heart will beat and burn,
And hang my wreath on this world-honored urn.
Nature, they say, doth dote,
And can not make a man
Save on some worn-out plan,
Repeating us by rote;
For him her old world molds aside she threw,
And, choosing sweet clay from the breast
Of the unexhausted West,
With stuff untainted, shaped a hero new,
Wise, steadfast in the strength of God, and true.

5

THE PRAISE OF LINCOLN

How beautiful to see
Once more a shepherd of mankind, indeed,
Who loved his charge, but never loved to lead;
One whose meek flock the people joyed to be,
Not lured by any cheat of birth,
But by his clean-grained human worth,
And brave old wisdom of sincerity!
They know that outward grace is dust;
They could not choose but trust
In that sure-footed mind's unfaltering skill,
And supple-tempered will
That bent like perfect steel to spring again and thrust.

His was no lonely mountain peak of mind,
Thrusting to thin air o'er our cloudy bars,
A sea mark now, now lost in vapors blind;
Broad prairie rather, genial, level lined,
Fruitful and friendly for all human kind,
Yet also nigh to heaven and loved of loftiest stars.
Nothing of Europe here,
Or, then, of Europe fronting mornward still,
Ere any names of serf or peer
Could Nature's equal scheme deface
And thwart her genial will;
Here was a type of the true elder race,
And one of Plutarch's men talked with us face to face.
I praise him not; it were too late;
And some innative weakness there must be
In him who condescends to victory
Such as the present gives and can not wait,
Safe in himself as in a fate.
So always firmly he:
He knew to bide his time,
And can his fame abide,
Still patient in his faith sublime,
Till the wise years decide.

6

THE PRAISE OF LINCOLN

Great captains with their guns and drums,
Disturb our judgment of the hour,
But at last Silence comes;
These all are gone, and, standing like a tower,
Our children shall behold his fame,
The kindly-earnest, brave, foreseeing man,
Sagacious, patient, dreading praise, not blame,
New birth of our new soil, the first American.

LINCOLN

James Whitcomb Riley

A PEACEFUL life;—just toil and rest—
 All his desire;—
To read the books he liked the best
 Beside the cabin fire—
God's word and man's;—to peer sometimes
 Above the page, in smouldering gleams,
And catch, like far heroic rhymes,
 The onmarch of his dreams.

A peaceful life;—to hear the low
 Of pastured herds,
Or woodman's axe that, blow on blow,
 Fell sweet as rhythmic words.
And yet there stirred within his breast
 A fateful pulse that, like a roll
Of drums, made high above his rest
 A tumult in his soul.

A peaceful life! . . . They haled him even
 As One was haled
Whose open palms were nailed toward Heaven
 When prayers nor aught availed.

And, lo, he paid the selfsame price
To lull a nation's awful strife
And will us, through the sacrifice
Of self, his peaceful life.

LINCOLN

Julia Ward Howe

THROUGH the dim pageant of the years
A wondrous tracery appears;
A cabin of the Western wild
Shelters to sleep a newborn child.

Nor nurse, nor parent dear can know
The way those infant feet must go;
And yet a nation's help and hope
Are sealed within that horoscope.

Beyond is toil for daily bread
And thought, to noble issues led,
And courage arming for the morn
For whose behest this man was born.

A man of homely, rustic ways,
Yet he achieves the forum's praise,
And soon earth's highest meed has won,
The seat and sway of Washington.

No throne of honors and delights;
Distrustful days and sleepless nights,
To struggle, suffer, and aspire,
Like Israel, led by cloud and fire.

8

THE PRAISE OF LINCOLN

A treacherous shot, a sob of rest,
A martyr's palm upon his breast,
A welcome from the glorious seat
Where blameless souls of heroes meet.

And thrilling through unmeasured days,
A song of gratitude and praise;
A cry that all the earth shall heed,
To God, who gave him for our need.

AN APPRECIATION OF LINCOLN

Robertus Love

SOMEWHAR down thar round Hodgenville, Kaintucky,
　Or tharabouts, a hundred year ago,
Was born a boy ye wouldn' thought was lucky;
　Looked like he never wouldn' have a show.
　　But . . . I don' know.
That boy was started middlin' well, I'm thinkin'.
His name? W'y, it was Abraham—Abe Lincoln.

Pore whites his folks was? Yes, as pore as any.
　Them pioneers, they wa'n't no plutocrats;
Belonged right down among the humble many,
　And no more property than dogs or cats.
　　But . . . maybe that's
As good a way as any for a startin'.
Abe Lincoln, he riz middlin' high, for sartin!

Somehow I've always had a sort o' sneakin'
　Idee that peddygrees is purty much
Like monkeys' tails—so long they're apt to weaken
　The yap that drags 'em round. No use for such!
　　But . . . beats the Dutch
How now and then a lad like little Aby
Grows up a president—or guvnor, maybe.

9

THE PRAISE OF LINCOLN

Abe Lincoln never had no reg'lar schoolin';
   He never quarterbacked nor pulled stroke oar,
Nor never spent his time and money foolin'
   With buried langwidges and ancient lore.
     But . . . Abe l'arned more
To set him forrerd in the human filin'
Than all the college fellers' kit and bilin'.

Abe Lincoln never did git hifalutin'—
   Not even thar in Washin'ton, D. C.
He jist kep' common, humble, ord'n'ry, suitin'
   His backwoods corn patch raisin' to a T.
     But . . . jiminy gee!
W'y, Abe was any statesman's peer and ekul
And wise as Solomon or old Ezekul.

I reckon, I'm a bit old-fashioned, maybe,
   But when I want a pattern for a man
I'm middlin' shore to measure Father Aby
   And cut to fit his homely human plan.
     And long's I can
I'm hootin' loud and rootin' proud, by hucky,
For that old boy from Hodgenville, Kaintucky.

LINCOLN

Samuel E. Kiser

New heroes rise above the toiling throng,
   And daily come resplendent into view,
   And pass again, remembered by a few,
To leave one form in bold relief and strong
That higher looms as ages march along;
   One name that lingers in the memory, too,
And singers through all time shall raise the song
And keep it swelling loud and ringing true!

THE PRAISE OF LINCOLN

Lo, where the feet of Lincoln passed, the earth
   Is sacred, where he knelt we set a shrine!
Oh, to have pressed his hand! That had sufficed
To make my children wonder at my worth—
   Yet, let them glory, since their land and mine
Hath reared the greatest martyr after Christ!

ABRAHAM LINCOLN

Virginia Frazer Boyle

(Written for the Centennial Celebration, February 12th, 1909, by
Invitation of the Philadelphia Brigade Association—Penna.)

"The mystic chords of memory, stretching from every battlefield
and patriot grave to every living heart and hearthstone, all over
this broad land, will yet swell the chorus of the Union, when again
touched, as surely they will be, by the angels of our better nature."—*Abraham Lincoln.*

No TRUMPET blared the word that he was born,
   Nor lightning flashed its symbols on the day;
And only Poverty and Fate pressed on,
   To serve as handmaids where he lowly lay.

No royal trappings fell to his rude part,—
   A simple hut and labor were its goal;
But Fate, stern-eyed, had held him to her heart,
   And left a greatness on his rugged soul.

And up from earth and toil, he slowly won,—
   Pressed by a bitterness he proudly spurned,
Till by grim courage, born from sun to sun,
   He turned defeat, as victory is turned.

Sired deep in destiny, he backward threw
   The old heredities that men have known;
And round his gaunt and homely form he drew
   The fierce white light that greatness makes its own.

11

THE PRAISE OF LINCOLN

Sad-eyed and wan, yet strong to do the right,—
  To clear the truth, as God gave him to see,
He held a raging country by his might,
  Before the iron hour of destiny.

Nor flame nor sword nor silver tongues availed
  To turn his passion from its steady flow;
The compact of the Fathers had not failed,—
  He would not let an angered people go!—

He stood in calm, while shaking chaos swept
  The Union,—North and South, in seething flood.
And on his knees the griefs of both he wept,—
  But kept unbroke, the compact sealed in blood.

He saw the sullen smoke of battle lift,
  That closed the carnage of the war of wars;
And on the height, hailed through the azure rift
  The flag whose folds have never dipped its stars.

But amnesty was in the conquering hand
  That yearned across the silent cannon's mouth;—
When with the knell that startled all the land,
  There died the last hope of the bleeding South!—

With gentle tread, time wears upon the past.
  The field of blood is dried, the waste is tilled;
And by the light of peace around them cast,
  Men read the earnest prophecy, fulfilled.

There is no woe in this broad land to-day,
  Held in the bonds of faith, forever one;
The golden glow of progress leads the way,
  Where once the guns of wrath have darkly shone.

THE PRAISE OF LINCOLN

Here rest their arms, while deathless glory tells
    The watch of time for all the true and brave,—
And here the grandeur of a Nation dwells,—
    The Union, that a Lincoln died to save!—

THE CENOTAPH OF LINCOLN

James T. McKay

And so they buried Lincoln? Strange and vain.
    Has any creature thought of Lincoln hid
    In any vault 'neath any coffin lid,
In all the years since that wild spring of pain?
'Tis false—he never in the grave hath lain.
    You could not bury him although you slid
    Upon his clay the Cheops Pyramid,
Or heaped it with the Rocky Mountain chain.
They slew themselves;—they but set Lincoln free.
    In all the earth his great heart beats as strong,
Shall beat while pulses throb to chivalry,
    And burn with hate of tyranny and wrong.
Whoever will may find him, anywhere
Save in the tomb. Not there—he is not there.

LINCOLN, THE MAN OF THE PEOPLE

Edwin Markham

When the Norn Mother saw the Whirlwind Hour
Greatening and darkening as it hurried on,
She left the Heaven of Heroes and came down
To make a man to meet the mortal need.
She took the tried clay of the common road—
Clay warm yet with the ancient heat of Earth,

THE PRAISE OF LINCOLN

Dashed through it all a strain of prophecy;
Tempered the heap with thrill of human tears;
Then mixed a laughter with the serious stuff.
Into the shape she breathed a flame to light
That tender, tragic, ever-changing face.
Here was a man to hold against the world,
A man to match the mountains and the sea.

The color of the ground was in him, the red earth;
The smack and tang of elemental things:
The rectitude and patience of the cliff;
The good-will of the rain that loves all leaves;
The friendly welcome of the wayside well;
The courage of the bird that dares the sea;
The gladness of the wind that shakes the corn;
The mercy of the snow that hides all scars;
The secrecy of streams that make their way
Beneath the mountain to the rifted rock;
The undelaying justice of the light
That gives as freely to the shrinking flower
As to the great oak flaring to the wind—
To the grave's low hill as to the Matterhorn
That shoulders out the sky.

                Sprung from the West,
The strength of virgin forests braced his mind,
The hush of spacious prairies stilled his soul.
Up from log cabin to the Capitol,
One fire was on his spirit, one resolve—
To send the keen ax to the root of wrong,
Clearing a free way for the feet of God.
And evermore he burned to do his deed
With the fine stroke and gesture of a king:
He built the rail-pile as he built the State,
Pouring his splendid strength through every blow,
The conscience of him testing every stroke,
To make his deed the measure of a man.

14

THE PRAISE OF LINCOLN

So came the Captain with the thinking heart;
And when the judgment thunders split the house,
Wrenching the rafters from their ancient rest,
He held the ridgepole up, and spiked again
The rafters of the Home.   He held his place—
Held the long purpose like a growing tree—
Held on through blame and faltered not at praise,
And when he fell in whirlwind, he went down
As when a lordly cedar, green with boughs,
Goes down with a great shout upon the hills,
And leaves a lonesome place against the sky.

IN MEMORIAM: ABRAHAM LINCOLN

Emily J. Bugbee

THERE'S a burden of grief on the breezes of spring,
And a song of regret from the bird on its wing;
There's a pall on the sunshine and over the flowers,
And a shadow of graves on these spirits of ours;
For a star hath gone out from the night of our sky,
On whose brightness we gazed as the war cloud rolled
      by;
So tranquil and steady and clear were its beams,
That they fell like a vision of peace on our dreams.

A heart that we knew had been true to our weal,
And a hand that was steadily guiding the wheel;
A name never tarnished by falsehood or wrong,
That had dwelt in our hearts like a soul-stirring song;
Ah, that pure, noble spirit has gone to its rest,
And the true hand lies nerveless and cold on his breast;
But the name and the memory, these never will die,
But grow brighter and dearer as ages go by.

15

THE PRAISE OF LINCOLN

Yet the tears of a nation fall over the dead,
Such tears as a nation before never shed,
For our cherished one fell by a dastardly hand,
A martyr to truth and the cause of the land;
And a sorrow has surged like the waves to the shore
When the breath of the tempest is sweeping them o'er;
And the heads of the lofty and lowly have bowed
As the shaft of the lightning sped out from the cloud.

Not gathered, like Washington, home to his rest,
When the sun of his life was far down in the West;
But stricken from earth in the midst of his years,
With the Canaan in view of his prayers and his tears;
And the people, whose hearts in the wilderness failed,
Sometimes, when the stars of their promise had paled,
Now stand by his side on the mount of his fame,
And yield him their hearts in a grateful acclaim.

Yet there on the mountain our leader must die,
With the fair land of promise spread out to his eye;
His work is accomplished, and what he has done
Will stand as a monument under the sun;
And his name, reaching down through the ages of time,
Will still through the years of eternity shine,
Like a star sailing on through the depths of the blue,
On whose brightness we gaze every evening anew.

His white tent is pitched on the beautiful plain,
Where the tumult of battle comes never again,
Where the smoke of the war cloud ne'er darkens the
        air,
Nor falls on the spirit a shadow of care.
The songs of the ransomed enrapture his ear,
And he heeds not the dirges that roll for him here;
In the calm of his spirit, so strange and sublime,
He is lifted far over the discords of time.

THE PRAISE OF LINCOLN

Then bear him home gently, great son of the West!
'Mid her fair blooming prairies lay Lincoln to rest;
From the nation who loves him she takes to her trust,
And will tenderly garner the consecrate dust.
A Mecca his grave to the people shall be,
A shrine evermore to the hearts of the free.

AT LINCOLN'S GRAVE

Maurice Thompson

MAY one who fought in honor for the South
Uncovered stand and sing by Lincoln's grave?
Why, if I shrank not at the cannon's mouth,
Nor swerved one inch for any battle-wave,
Should I now tremble in this quiet close,
Hearing the prairie wind go lightly by
From billowy plains of grass and miles of corn,
　　　　While out of deep repose,
The great sweet spirit lifts itself on high
And broods above our land this summer morn?

I, mindful of a dark and bitter past,
And of its clashing hopes and raging hates,
Still, standing here, invoke a love so vast
It cancels all and all obliterates,
Save love itself, which can not harbor wrong;
Oh, for a voice of boundless melody,
A voice to fill heaven's hollow to the brim
　　　　With one brave burst of song,
Stronger than tempest, nobler than the sea,
That I might lend it to a song of him!

17

THE PRAISE OF LINCOLN

Meseems I feel his presence. Is he dead?
Death is a word. He lives and grander grows.
At Gettysburg he bows his bleeding head;
He spreads his arms where Chickamauga flows,
As if to clasp old soldiers to his breast,
Of South or North, no matter which they be,
Not thinking of what uniform they wore,—
   His heart the palimpsest
Record on record of humanity,
Where love is first and last for evermore.

His humor, born of virile opulence,
Stung like a pungent sap or wild-fruit zest,
And satisfied a universal sense
Of manliness, the strongest and the best;
A soft Kentucky strain was in his voice,
And the Ohio's deeper boom was there,
With some wild accents of old Wabash days,
   And winds of Illinois;
And when he spoke he took us unaware,
With his high courage and unselfish ways.

He was the North, the South, the East, the West,
The thrall, the master, all of us in one;
There was no section that he held the best;
His love shone as impartial as the sun;
And so revenge appealed to him in vain,
He smiled at it as at a thing forlorn,
And gently put it from him, rose and stood
   A moment's space in pain,
Remembering the prairies and the corn
And the glad voices of the field and wood.

Annealed in white-hot fire, he bore the test
Of every strain temptation could invent,—
Hard points of slander, shivered on his breast,
Fell at his feet, and envy's blades were bent

In his bare hands and lightly cast aside;
He would not wear a shield; no selfish aim
Guided one thought of all those trying hours;
       No breath of pride,
No pompous striving for the pose of fame
Weakened one stroke of all his noble powers.

PRESIDENT LINCOLN'S GRAVE

Caroline A. Mason

LAY his dear ashes where ye will,—
On southern slope or western hill;
And build above his sacred name
Your proudest monument of fame;
Yet still his grave our hearts shall be;
His monument a people free!
    Sing sweet, sing low;
    We loved him so!
His grave a nation's heart shall be,
His monument a people free!

Wave, prairie winds! above his sleep
Your mournful dirges, long and deep;
Proud marble! o'er his virtues raise
The tribute of your glittering praise;
Yet still his grave our hearts shall be;
His monument a people free!
    Sing sweet, sing low;
    We loved him so!
His grave a nation's heart shall be;
His monument a people free!

So just, so merciful, so wise,
Ye well may shrine him where he lies;
So simply good, so great the while
Ye well may raise the marble pile;

Yet still his grave our hearts shall be;
His monument a people free!
   Sing sweet, sing low;
   We loved him so!
His grave a nation's heart shall be;
His monument a people free!

LINCOLN

Authorship Unknown

LINCOLN! When men would name a man,
   Just, unperturbed, magnanimous,
Tried in the lowest seat of all,
   Tried in the chief seat of the house—

Lincoln! When men would name a man
   Who wrought the great work of his age,
Who fought and fought the noblest fight,
   And marshaled it from stage to stage,

Victorious, out of dusk and dark,
   And into dawn and on till day,
Most humble when the pæans rang,
   Least rigid when the enemy lay

Prostrated for his feet to tread—
   This name of Lincoln will they name,
A name revered, a name of scorn,
   Of scorn to sundry, not to fame.

Lincoln, the man who freed the slave;
   Lincoln whom never self enticed;
Slain Lincoln, worthy found to die
   A soldier of his Captain Christ.

AT LINCOLN'S TOMB

Robertus Love

(Being the Reminiscences of the Honorable Jason Pettigrew, of
Calhoun County, Illinois, in 1895)

ABE LINCOLN? Wull, I reckon! Not a mile f'om
    where we be,
Right here in Springfiel', Illinoise, Abe used to room
    with me.
He represented Sangamon, I tried it for Calhoun,
And me and Abe was cronies then; I'll not forgit it
    soon.

I'll not forgit them happy days we used to sort o' batch
Together in a little room that didn't have no latch
To keep the other fellers out that liked to come and
    stay
And hear them dasted funny things Abe Lincoln used
    to say.

Them days Abe Lincoln and myself was pore as any-
    thing;
Job's turkey wasn't porer, but we used to laff and sing,
And Abe was clean chuck full o' fun, but he was sharp
    as tacks,
For that there comic face o' his'n was fortyfied with
    fac's.

Some fellers used to laff at Abe because his boots and
    pants
Appeared to be on distant terms, but when he'd git a
    chance
He'd give 'em sich a drubbin' that they'd clean forgit
    his looks,
For Abe made up in common sense the things he lacked
    in books.

THE PRAISE OF LINCOLN

Wull, nex' election I got beat, and Abe come back
    alone;
I kep' a-clinkin' on the farm, pervidin' for my own.
You see, I had a woman and two twins that called me
    paw,
And Abe he kep' a-clinkin', too, at politics and law.

I didn't hear much more of Abe out there in old Cal-
    houn,
For I was out o' politics and kinder out o' chune
With things that happened, but 'way back I'd named
    my two twin boys—
One Abraham, one Lincoln—finest team in Illinoise.

Wull, here one day I read that Abe's among the can-
    didates
(My old friend Abe!) for president o' these United
    States.
And, though I had the rheumatiz and felt run-down
    and blue,
I entered politics ag'in and helped to pull him through.

And when nex' spring he called for men to fetch their
    grit and guns
And keep the ship o' state afloat I sent him both my
    sons,
And would 'a' gone myself and loved to make the bul-
    lets whiz
'F it hadn't b'en I couldn't walk account o' rheumatiz.

Wull, Abe—my little Abe, I mean—he started out
    with Grant;
They buried him at Shiloh. . . . Excuse me, but I
    can't
Help feelin' father-like, you know, for them was likely
    boys;
The' wasn't two another sich that went f'om Illinoise.

And Lincoln—my son Lincoln—he went on by his-
    self,
A-grievin' for his brother Abe they'd laid upon the
    shelf,
And when he come to Vicksburg he was all thrashed
    out and sick,
And yit when there was fightin' Link fit right in the
    thick.

One night afore them Johnnies' guns my pore boy
    went to sleep
On picket dooty. . . . No, sir; 'tain't the shame
    that makes me weep.
It's how Abe Lincoln, president, at Washin'ton, D. C.,
Had time to ricolleck the days he used to room with
    me!

For don't you know I wrote to him they'd sentenced to
    be shot
His namesake, Lincoln Pettigrew, in shame to die and
    rot,
The son o' his old crony and the last o' my twin boys
He used to plague me so about at Springfiel', Illinoise.

Did he? Did Abe? Wull, now, he sent a telegraph so
    quick
It burnt them bottles on the poles and made the light-
    nin' sick!
"I pardon Lincoln Pettigrew. A. Lincoln, President."
The boy has got that paper yit, the telegraph Abe sent.

I guess I knowed Abe Lincoln, and now I've come
    down here—
Firs' time I be'n in Springfiel' for nigh on sixty year—
To see his grave and tombstone, because . . . be-
    cause, you see,
We legislated in cahoots, Abe Lincoln did, and me.

ON THE LIFE-MASK OF ABRAHAM LINCOLN

Richard Watson Gilder

THIS bronze doth keep the very form and mold
    Of our great martyr's face. Yes, this is he:
    That brow all wisdom, all benignity;
    That human, humorous mouth; those cheeks that
        hold
Like some harsh landscape all the summer's gold;
    That spirit fit for sorrow, as the sea
    For storms to beat on; the lone agony
    Those silent, patient lips too well foretold.
Yes, this is he who ruled a world of men
    As might some prophet of the elder day—
    Brooding above the tempest and the fray
With deep-eyed thought and more than mortal ken.
    A power was his beyond the touch of art
    Or armed strength—his pure and mighty heart.

THE GRAVE OF LINCOLN

Edna Dean Proctor

Now must the storied Potomac
    Laurels for ever divide,
Now to the Sangamon fameless
    Give of its century's pride.
Sangamon, stream of the prairies,
    Placidly westward that flows,
Far in whose city of silence
    Calm he has sought his repose.
Over our Washington's river
    Sunrise beams rosy and fair,
Sunset on Sangamon fairer—
    Father and martyr lies there.

24

THE PRAISE OF LINCOLN

Kings under pyramids slumber,
    Sealed in the Lybian sands;
Princes in gorgeous cathedrals
    Decked with the spoil of the lands.
Kinglier, princelier sleeps he
    Couched 'mid the prairies serene,
Only the turf and the willow
    Him and God's heaven between!
Temple nor column to cumber
    Verdure and bloom of the sod—
So, in the vale by Beth-peor,
    Moses was buried of God.

Break into blossom, O prairies!
    Snowy and golden and red;
Peers of the Palestine lilies
    Heap for your glorious dead!
Roses as fair as of Sharon,
    Branches as stately as palm,
Odors as rich as the spices—
    Cassia and aloes and balm—
Mary the loved and Salome,
    All with a gracious accord,
Ere the first glow of the morning
    Brought to the tomb of the Lord.

Wind of the West! breathe around him
    Soft as the saddened air's sigh
When to the summit of Pisgah
    Moses had journeyed to die.
Clear as its anthem that floated
    Wide o'er the Moabite plain,
Low with the wail of the people
    Blending its burdened refrain.

25

THE PRAISE OF LINCOLN

Rarer, O Wind! and diviner,—
    Sweet as the breeze that went by,
When, over Olivet's mountain,
    Jesus was lost in the sky.

Not for thy sheaves and savannas
    Crown we thee, proud Illinois!
Here in his grave is thy grandeur;
    Born of his sorrow thy joy.
Only the tomb by Mount Zion
    Hewn for the Lord do we hold
Dearer than his in thy prairies,
    Girdled with harvests of gold.
Still for the world, through the ages
    Wreathing with glory his brow,
He shall be Liberty's Savior—
    Freedom's Jerusalem thou!

THE HAND OF LINCOLN

Edmund Clarence Stedman

Look on this cast, and know the hand
    That bore a nation in its hold;
From this mute witness understand
    What Lincoln was—how large of mold.

The man who sped the woodman's team,
    And deepest sunk the plowman's share,
And pushed the laden raft astream,
    Of fate before him unaware.

This was the hand that knew to swing
    The axe—since thus would Freedom train
Her son—and made the forest ring,
    And drove the wedge, and toiled amain.

THE PRAISE OF LINCOLN

Firm hand, that loftier office took,
  A conscious leader's will obeyed,
And, when men sought his word and look,
  With steadfast might the gathering swayed.

No courtier's, toying with a sword,
  Nor minstrel's, laid across a lute;
A chief's, uplifted to the Lord
  When all the kings of earth were mute!

The hand of Anak, sinewed strong,
  The fingers that on greatness clutch;
Yet, lo! the marks their lines along
  Of one who strove and suffered much.

For here in knotted cord and vein,
  I trace the varying chart of years;
I know the troubled heart, the strain,
  The weight of Atlas—and the tears.

Again I see the patient brow
  That palm erewhile was wont to press;
And now 'tis furrowed deep, and now
  Made smooth with hope and tenderness.

For something of a formless grace
  This molded outline plays about;
A pitying flame, beyond our trace,
  Breathes like a spirit, in and out.

The love that casts an aureole
  Round one who, longer to endure,
Called mirth to ease his ceaseless dole,
  Yet kept his nobler purpose sure.

THE PRAISE OF LINCOLN

Lo, as I gaze, the statured man,
  Built up from yon large hand, appears;
A type that nature wills to plan
  But once in all a people's years.

What better than this voiceless cast
  To tell of such a one as he,
Since through its living semblance passed
  The thought that bade a race be free.

THE LIFE-MASK OF ABRAHAM LINCOLN

Stuart Sterne

(At the National Museum in Washington)

AH, countless wonders brought from every zone,
  Not all your wealth could turn the heart away
  From that one semblance of our common clay,
  The brow whereon the precious life long flown
Leaving a homely glory all its own,
  Seems still to linger, with a mournful play
  Of light and shadow!—His, who held a sway
  And power of magic to himself unknown,
Through what is granted but God's chosen few,
  Earth's crownless, yet anointed kings,—a soul
  Divinely simple and sublimely true
In that unconscious greatness that shall bless
  This petty world while stars their courses roll,
  Whose finest flower is *self-forgetfulness.*

THE LIBERATOR

Horace Spencer Fiske

(Saint Gaudens' Lincoln, Lincoln Park, Chicago)

UPRISEN from his fascéd chair of state,
  Above his riven people bending grave,
  His heart upon the sorrow of the slave,
Stands simply strong the kindly man of fate,
By war's deep bitterness and brothers' hate
  Untouched he stands, intent alone to save
  What God Himself and human justice gave;
The right of men to freedom's fair estate.
In human strength he towers almost divine,
  His mighty shoulders bent with breaking care,
His thought-worn face with sympathies grown fine;
  And as men gaze, their hearts as oft declare
That this is he whom all their hearts enshrine—
This man that saved a race from slow despair.

LINCOLN IN BRONZE

Robertus Love

(In Lincoln Park, Chicago)

HERE do I look upon historic form
  Fashioned in bronze grown cold, but glowing yet—
  In our Columbia's memory-casket set
A sovereign jewel. Earth's unconscious storm
May beat upon and work the statue harm;
  Old Time may topple it without regret.
  Perish the bronze! But we will not forget
The great heart for its brothers beating warm.

29

THE PRAISE OF LINCOLN

The hand of Lincoln, bronzed by honest toil
   That drove the ax to fell the forest oak,
Then working up amid the world's turmoil,
   At one proud blow four million fetters broke:
It is not dust—still does it reach and clasp
Past, Present, Future, in its kindly grasp.

THE EMANCIPATION GROUP

John Greenleaf Whittier

(Park Square, Boston)

AMIDST thy sacred effigies
   Of old renown give place,
O city, Freedom-loved! to his
   Whose hand unchained a race.

Take the worn frame, that rested not
   Save in a martyr's grave;
The care-lined face, that none forgot,
   Bent to the kneeling slave.

Let man be free! The mighty word
   He spoke was not his own;
An impulse from the Highest stirred
   These chiseled lips alone.

The cloudy sign, the fiery guide,
   Along his pathway ran,
And Nature, through his voice, denied
   The ownership of man.

We rest in peace where these sad eyes
   Saw peril, strife and pain;
His was the nation's sacrifice,
   And ours the priceless gain.

THE PRAISE OF LINCOLN

O symbol of God's will on earth
  As it is done above!
Bear witness to the cost and worth
  Of justice and of love.

Stand in thy place and testify
  To coming ages long,
That truth is stronger than a lie,
  And righteousness than wrong.

ENGLAND'S SORROW

Authorship Unknown—From London Fun

THE hand of an assassin, glowing red,
  Shot like a firebrand through the western sky;
And stalwart Abraham Lincoln now is dead!
  Oh, felon heart that thus could basely dye
The name of Southerner with murderous gore!
  Could such a spirit come from mortal womb?
And what possessed it that not heretofore
  It linked its coward mission with the tomb?
Lincoln! thy fame shall sound through many an age,
  To prove that genius lives in humble birth;
Thy name shall sound upon historic page,
  For 'midst thy faults we all esteemed thy worth.
Gone art thou now! no more 'midst angry heat
  Shall thy calm spirit rule the surging tide,
Which rolls where two contending nations meet,
  To still the passion and to curb the pride.
Nations have looked and seen the fate of kings,
  Protestors, Emperors, and such like men;
Behold the man whose dirge all Europe sings,
  Now past the eulogy of mortal pen!
He, like a lighthouse fell athwart the strand;
Let curses rest upon the assassin's hand!

WE TALKED OF LINCOLN

Edward William Thomson

WE talked of Abraham Lincoln in the night,
Ten fur-coat men on North Saskatchewan's plain—
Pure zero cold and all the prairie white—
Englishman, Scotchman, Scandinavian, Dane,
Two Irish, four Canadians—all for gain
Of food and raiment, children, parents, wives,
Living the hardest life that man survives,
And secret proud because it was so hard
Exploring, camping, axing, faring lean.—
Month in and out no creature had we seen
Except our burdened dogs, gaunt foxes gray,
Hard-feathered grouse that shot would seldom slay,
Slinking coyotes, plumy-trailing owls,
Stark Indians warm in rabbit-blanket cowls,
And, still as shadows in their deep-tracked yard,
The dun vague moose we startled from our way.

We talked of Abraham Lincoln in the night
Around our fire of tamarac crackling fierce.
Yet dim, like moon and stars, in that vast light
Boreal, bannery, shifting quick to pierce
Ethereal blanks of Space with falchion streams
Transfigured wondrous into quivering beams
From Forms enormous—marching through the sky
To dissolution and new majesty.
And speech was low around our bivouac fire,
Since in our inmost heart of hearts there grew
The sense of mortal feebleness, to see
Those silent miracles of Might on high
Seemingly done for only such as we
In sign how nearer Death and Doom we drew,
While in the ancient tribal-soul we knew

32

THE PRAISE OF LINCOLN

Our old hardfaring father-Vikings' dreams
Of Odin at Valhalla's open door,
Where they might see the Battle-father's face
Glowing at last, when Life and Toil were o'er,
Were they but staunch-enduring in their place.

We talked of Abraham Lincoln in the night.—
Oh, sweet and strange to hear the hard-hand men
Old-Abeing him, like half the world of yore
In years when Grant's and Lee's young soldiers bore
Rifle and steel, and proud that heroes live
When folks their lives to Labor mostly give.
And strange and sweet to hear their voices call
Him "Father Abraham," though no man of all
Was born within the Nation of his birth,
It was as if they felt that all the Earth
Possess of right Earth's greatest common man,
Her sanest, wisest, simplest, steadiest son,
To whom The Father's children all were one,
And Pomp and Vanities as motes that danced
In the clear sunshine where his humor glanced.

We talked of Abraham Lincoln in the night
Until one spoke, *"We yet may see his face."*
Whereon the fire crackled loud through space
Of human silence, while eyes reverent
Toward the auroral miracle were bent
Till from the trancing Glory spirits came
Within our semicircle round the flame,
And drew us closer-ringed, until we could
Feel the kind touch of vital brotherhood
Which Father Abraham Lincoln thought so good.

33

WASHINGTON AND LINCOLN

Authorship Unknown

ONE forged the links that welded fast
The nation's fame that it might last
   Forever and a day;
The other with his might and main
Did rivet it when rent in twain—
   His name will live for aye!

Hail, Washington! and Lincoln, hail!
Your glory shall not fade nor fail,
   The Stars and Stripes shall wave
Resplendent o'er our crags and shores,
Majestic as the eagle soars—
   Triumphant o'er the grave!

PUNCH'S APOLOGY

Tom Taylor

(Abraham Lincoln, Foully Assassinated April, 1865)

You lay a wreath on murdered Lincoln's bier,
   You, who, with mocking pencil wont to trace
Broad, for the self-complacent sneer,
   His length of shambling limb, his furrowed face.

His gaunt, gnarled hands, his unkempt, bristling hair,
   His garb uncouth, his bearing ill at ease,
His lack of all we prize as debonair,
   Of power or will to shine, of art to please.

THE PRAISE OF LINCOLN

You, whose smart pen backed up the pencil's laugh,
   Judging each step as though the way were plain;
Reckless, so it could point its paragraph
   Of chief's perplexity, or people's pain.

Beside this corpse, that bears for winding sheet
   The Stars and Stripes he lived to rear anew,
Between the mourners at his head and feet,
   Say, scurril jester, is there room for you?

Yes, he had lived to shame me from my sneer,
   To lame my pencil and confute my pen—
To make me own this hind of princes peer,
   This rail splitter, as true-born king of men.

My shallow judgment I had learned to rue,
   Noting how to occasion's height he rose,
How his quaint wit made home truth seem more true,
   How iron-like, his temper grew by blows.

How humble, yet how hopeful he could be;
   How in good fortune and in ill the same;
Nor bitter in success, nor boastful he,
   Thirsty for gold nor feverish for fame.

He went about his work—such work as few
   Ever had laid on head, and heart, and hand—
As one who knows, where there's a task to do,
   Man's honest will must Heaven's good grace command.

Who trusts the strength will with the burden grow,
   That God makes instruments to work His will,
If but that will we can arrive to know,
   Nor tamper with the weights of good and ill.

THE PRAISE OF LINCOLN

So he went forth to battle, on the side
  That he felt clear was Liberty's and Right's,
As in his peasant boyhood he had plied
  His warfare with rude Nature's thwarting mights—

The uncleared forest, the unbroken soil,
  The iron bark that turns the lumberer's axe,
The rapid, that o'erbears the boatman's toil,
  The prairie, hiding the mazed wanderer's tracks,

The ambushed Indian, and the prowling bear—
  Such were the needs that helped his youth to train;
Rough culture—but such trees large fruit may bear,
  If but their stocks be of right girth and grain.

So he grew up a destined work to do,
  And lived to do it; four long, suffering years'
Ill fate, ill feeling, ill report, lived through,
  And then he heard the hisses change to cheers,

The taunts to tribute, the abuse to praise,
  And took both with the same unwavering mood;
Till, as he came on light, from darkling days,
  And seemed to touch the goal from where he stood.

A felon hand, between the goal and him,
  Reached from behind his back, a trigger pressed—
And those perplexed and patient eyes were dim,
  Those gaunt, long laboring limbs were laid to rest!

The words of mercy were upon his lips,
  Forgiveness in his heart and on his pen,
When this vile murderer brought swift eclipse
  To thoughts of peace on earth, good will to men.

THE PRAISE OF LINCOLN

The old world and the new, from sea to sea,
    Utter one voice of sympathy and shame!
Sore heart, so stopped when it at last beat high,
    Sad life, cut short just as its triumph came.

A deed accursed! Strokes have been struck before
    By the assassin's hand, whereof men doubt
If more of horror or disgrace they bore;
    But thy foul crime, like Cain's, stands darkly out.

Vile hand, that brandest murder on a strife,
    Whate'er its grounds, stoutly and nobly striven;
And with the martyr's crown crownest a life
    With much to praise, little to be forgiven.

ABRAHAM LINCOLN

Mary Livingston Burdick

SAFE in Fame's gallery through all the years,
    Our dearest picture hangs, your steadfast face,
    Whose eyes hold all the pathos of the race
Redeemed by you from Servitude's sad tears.

And how redeemed? With agony of grief;
    With ceaseless labor in war's lurid light;
    With such deep anguish in each lonely night,
Your soul sweat very blood ere came relief.

What crown have you who bore that cross below?
    O faithful one, what is your life above?
    Is there a higher gift in God's pure love
Than to have lived on earth as Man of Woe?

37

THE COMING OF LINCOLN

Edwin Markham

Men saw no portents on that winter night
A hundred years ago.   No omens flared
Above that rail-built cabin with one door,
And windowless to all the peering stars.
They laid him in the hollow of a log,
Humblest of cradles, save that other one—
The manger in the stall at Bethlehem.

No portents! yet with whisper and alarm
The Evil Powers that dread the nearing feet
Of heroes held a council in that hour;
And sent three fates to darken that low door,
To baffle and beat back the heaven-sent child.
Three were the fates—gaunt Poverty that chains,
Gray Drudgery that grinds the hope away,
And gaping Ignorance that starves the soul.

They came with secret laughters to destroy.
Ever they dogged him, counting every step,
Waylaid his youth and struggled for his life.
They came to master, but he made them serve.
And from the wrestle with the destinies,
He rose with all his energies aglow.

For God, upon whose steadfast shoulders rest
These governments of ours, had not forgot.
He needed for His purposes a voice,
A voice to be a clarion on the wind,
Crying the word of freedom to dead hearts,
The word the centuries had waited for.

THE PRAISE OF LINCOLN

So hidden in the West, God shaped His man.
There in the unspoiled solitudes he grew,
Unwarped by culture and uncramped by creed;
Keeping his course courageous and alone,
As goes the Mississippi to the sea.
His daring spirit burst the narrow bounds,
Rose resolute; and like the sea-called stream,
He tore new channels where he found no way.

The tools were his first teachers, sternly kind.
The plow, the scythe, the maul, the echoing axe
Taught him their homely wisdom and their peace.
He had the plain man's genius—common sense,
Yet rage for knowledge drove his mind afar;
He fed his spirit with the bread of books,
And slaked his thirst at all the wells of thought.

But most he read the heart of common man,
Scanned all its secret pages stained with tears,
Saw all the guile, saw all the piteous pain;
And yet could keep the smile about his lips,
Love and forgive, see all and pardon all;
His only fault, the fault that some of old
Laid even on God—that he was ever wont
To bend the law to let his mercy out.

LINCOLN

From the American Magazine

IN him distilled and potent the choice essence of a race!
Far back the Puritans—stern and manful visionaries,
Repressed poets, flushed with dreams of glowing theol-
    ogies!
Each new succession, out of border hardship,

39

Refined to human use the initial rigor of the breed,
Passing to the next the unconscious possession of a
    perfecting soul!
Each forest clearing gave something of neighborly
    grace,
The rude play of cabin-bred natural people something
    of humor,
Each mountain home something of inner daring,
Each long-wandering life something of patience and
    hope!
In the open, far-seen nature gradually chiseled
The deepening wistful eyes.
Each axman and each plowman added
Another filament of ruggedness;
Unknowing minds dumbly cried for liberty;
Mute hearts strove against injustice. . . .
At last was ready the alembic, where Nature stored
    and set apart
Each generation's finest residue,
Waiting for the hour of perfect mixture—
And then the Miracle!

ABRAHAM LINCOLN

Fred Clare Baldwin

WITH Humor's wand in hands to hardship used
    He changed the face of poverty's estate;
    At Wisdom's fount he drank insatiate;
O'er Destiny's dark sayings deeply mused:
Of large ambition let him be accused;
    Though ne'er will our full tide of joy abate
    That in the mold which cast a soul so great
Were heart and conscience with ambition fused:
As high in honor as in stature tall,
    In vision broader than the plains he trod,

THE PRAISE OF LINCOLN

As firm in courage as the buttressed wall,
  This child of genius was the friend of God;
And unto him the martyr's task was given,
To reunite a realm by hatred riven.

THE PROCLAMATION

Charles Godfrey Leland

Now who has done the greatest deed
  Which History has ever known?
And who in Freedom's direst need
  Became her bravest champion?
Who a whole continent set free?
  Who killed the curse and broke the ban
Which made a lie of liberty?
  You, Father Abraham—you're the man!

The deed is done. Millions have yearned
  To see the spear of Freedom cast.
The dragon roared and writhed and burned:
  You've smote him full and square at last.
O Great and True! You do not know—
  You can not tell—you can not feel
How far through time your name must go,
Honored by all men, high or low,
  Where Freedom's votaries kneel.

This wide world takes in many a tongue—
  This world boasts many a noble state;
In all your praises will be sung—
  In all the great will call you great.
Freedom! where'er that word is known—
  On silent shore, by sounding sea,
'Mid millions, or in deserts lone—
  Your noble name shall ever be.

41

THE PRAISE OF LINCOLN

The word is out, the deed is done,
　The spear is cast, dread no delay;
When such a steed is fairly gone,
　Fate never fails to find a way.
Hurrah! hurrah! the track is clear,
　We know your policy and plan;
We'll stand by you through every year;
　Now, Father Abraham, you're our man.

TO THE SPIRIT OF ABRAHAM
LINCOLN

Richard Watson Gilder

(Reunion at Gettysburg, 1888)

SHADE of our greatest, O look down to-day!
　Here the long, dread midsummer battle roared,
　And brother in brother plunged the accursed
　　sword;—
　Here foe meets foe once more in proud array
Yet not as once to harry and to slay
　But to strike hands, and with sublime accord
　Weep tears heroic for the souls that soared
　Quick from earth's carnage to the starry way.
Each fought for what he deemed the people's good,
　And proved his bravery with his offered life,
　And sealed his honor with his outpoured blood;
But the Eternal did direct the strife,
　And on this sacred field one patriot host
　Now calls thee father,—dear, majestic ghost!

THE FAME OF LINCOLN

A. Dallas Williams

WHEREVER men are civilized they know
  The name of him who gave his life to save
Our seething nation from impending woe,
  And found an honored but untimely grave.
Where'er the English tongue is spoken, there
  The name of Lincoln finds unstinted praise—
This shoulder-stooped, this toil-worn son of care,
  Who bore our burdens through unhappy days.

The name of Lincoln, all around the world,
  Is on the lips of statesman, slave, and king;
Where'er the flag of Freedom is unfurled,
  They know of Lincoln's toil and suffering,
They know of Lincoln's care and sacrifice,
  In all the nations underneath the skies;
Beneath the tropic sun, or 'midst the ice
  Of Arctic fields, deservèd fame ne'er dies.

Who can forget the patience, hope, and love
  That filled his heart through all the surging years
Of civil strife? the toil and grief thereof,
  The faith that led him on through falling tears?
Cheer for the friend, forgiveness for the foe,
  With aught of malice in his heart for none;
And when at last the writhing years of woe
  Were o'er, rejoicing that the strife was done.

Who can forget the cruel jeers and sneers
  Of those who should have helped, but criticized?
His heart was filled with pity, not with fears,
  Nor by their taunts and threats was he surprised;

43

THE PRAISE OF LINCOLN

With courage, calm, unfaltering as dawn,
  He stood, while friends and counsellors reviled;
He did the nearest duty, trusting on,
  And when rage changed to love, he simply smiled.

A loyal people have enshrined the great
  And patriotic statesman in their hearts;
Their love for him does not, can not abate;
  In homes and offices, in fields and marts,
His name is reverenced; both high and low,
  Men, women, children, join in the applause;
Yea, countless thousands worthy praise bestow
  On him who bravely toiled in Freedom's cause.

His fame endures—not like the fame of some,
  Whose names on every tongue applause invite,
And then the people suddenly are dumb;
  Like Jonah's gourd, which perished in a night,
Their fame is dead, and they are left in woe—
  The years but add fresh laurels to his name,
And like the mighty oaks which stately grow,
  So grows this patient man's undying fame.

LINCOLN

Richard Wightman

(1861-1865)

AND he was once a babe, little and like any other,
Wan, slow-eyed, knowing not his mother, knowing
    only her breasts,
Sleeping in the day, showing no hint of stature or of
    power!
What recked he that the walls about were less than
    palace walls,

44

THE PRAISE OF LINCOLN

Or that the snow, sifting upon him through the log-
    crevices,
Was not the dust of warm and gentle stars?
Rude-handed they who tended him—rough miners
    with a Kohinoor—
And yet were they the tools of God to help that babe
    to be!

Then sun succeeded sun, and to the wid'ning eyes of
    Youth
Far heights on heights stood clear,
Topped by a nameless glory to be won
By life and love and tireless trust in Right,
And patient toil and fearless grapple with the Wrong.
'Twas but the vision of a dreamful boy,
But in it surely lay the unity of States,
The lengthened gleam of all the Flag's fair stars,
And justice done to men—some white, some black,
The owners and the owned,
But bondaged all until the great Decree!

And oh, the soul of him
So stalwartly embarred within its clay,
Yet roaming far, halting not upon the shores of his
    America,
Crossing seas and deserts to set up its claim
Of universal kinship!
We say we are his people—proudly we say it and with
    reverence—
But in his heart he kept all men and fathered them with
    tenderness.
Almost it seemed as if from out his loins—
This great parental man—the race had sprung!
He knew no couch of down, no viands rare, no easy
    leveled way.

Lonely he fought his fight, and gained the meed of
    Wisdom,
Insignia of Poise, and Love's gemmed chaplet, fade-
    less through the years.
We say that he was born, and date his death,
But while the light seeks out the vales, and darkness
    holds them close
This man shall be!

ABRAHAM LINCOLN

Eugene J. Hall

O HONORED name, revered and undecaying,
    Engraven on each heart, O soul sublime!
That, like a planet through the heavens straying,
    Outlives the wreck of time!

O rough, strong soul, your noble self-possession
    Is unforgotten.   Still your work remains.
You freed from bondage and from vile oppression
    A race in clanking chains.

O furrowed face, beloved by all the nation!
    O tall, gaunt form, to memory fondly dear!
O firm, bold hand, our strength and our salvation!
    O heart that knew no fear!

Lincoln, your manhood shall survive for ever,
    Shedding a fadeless halo 'round your name;
Urging men on, with wise and strong endeavor
    To bright and honest fame!

Through years of care, to rest and joy a stranger,
    You saw complete the work you had begun;
Thoughtless of threats, nor heeding death or danger,
    You toiled till all was done.

THE PRAISE OF LINCOLN

You freed the bondman from his iron master,
  You broke the strong and cruel chains he wore;
You saved the ship of state from foul disaster,
  And brought her safe to shore.

You fell! An anxious nation's hopes seemed blighted,
  While millions shuddered at your dreadful fall;
But God is good! His wondrous hand has righted
  And reunited all.

You fell, but in your death you were victorious;
  To molder in the tomb your form has gone,
While through the world your great soul grows more
        glorious
  As years go gliding on.

All hail, great chieftain! Long will sweetly cluster
  A thousand memories 'round your sacred name,
Nor time nor death shall dim the spotless luster
  That shines upon your fame.

ON A PICTURE OF LINCOLN

John Vance Cheney

I READ once more this care-worn, patient face,
  And learn anew that sorrow is the dower
Of him that sinks himself to lift his race
  Into the seat of peace and power.

How beautiful the homely features grow,
  How soft the light from out the mild, sad eyes,
The gleam from deeps of grief the soul must know,
  To be so great,—so kind, so wise!

47

LINCOLN AT GETTYSBURG

Mary M. Adams

A NATION'S voice, a nation's praise,
  Above its honored dead!
The spot where on eventful days
  Its heroes fought and bled!
The spot where Freedom's spirit spoke
  In words sublime and true,
And where her trumpet tone awoke
  The old song and the new!

The old song with the newer strain,
  To make the first complete
With melody that lives again
  Through victory and defeat!
O sacred spot! thrice sacred now,
  As years thy record prove!
Before thy shrine all patriots bow,
  These shrines all doubts remove!

The patriot's heart with ardor glows,
  Remembering proffered lives;
He hears, in one strong breeze that blows,
  "Life goes, but love survives"—
The love that stirs a nation's heart,
  And bears a nation's fame
Wherever brave deeds have a part,
  And men such deeds proclaim.

He knows its thrilling music tells
  Of those who fell asleep,
And here found tomb, while muffled bells
  A nation's birthday keep.

48

THE PRAISE OF LINCOLN

He hears as well the tender moan
   That in its cadence sings
For those who sit henceforth alone,
   Whose muffled bell still rings.

He hears the added strain it bears
   For all who bravely fought,
For him who in the silence wears
   The scars the battle brought—
Who wears them with a hero's might,
   And honors still the hour
That won a nation's priceless right,
   And proved a nation's dower!

He hears it when it brings the name
   That won a martyr's crown,
Our glorious chief, whose stainless fame
   His country's best renown!
It brings the matchless words he said,
   Standing above their sod,
In hour whose burning import led
   A people nearer God.

It is not ours to dedicate
   This piece of earth so dear,
Nor is it ours to consecrate
   The deeds men witnessed here;
That has been done by those who died,
   On nation's altar slain;
They have these hillsides sanctified;
   Oh, prove it not in vain!

Great leader true! throughout all time
   The world will hear thy voice;
Because of thee a holier clime
   Bids liberty rejoice!

THE PRAISE OF LINCOLN

'Twas fitting you should tell of those
    Who wrote in blood their song,
And here thy nobler thought disclose
    How nations shall be strong!

How brave men shall perpetuate
    The freedom bravely won,
Forbid that treason desecrate
    What loyal sires begun;
And here on this great field to-day,
    In memory of thy birth,
Let nation's love its tribute pay,
    And echo round the earth!

But let our labor reach the height
    The larger manhood saw;
That broad humanity whose light
    Was Thy diviner law;
That law whose good is absolute,
    Whose mandate strong and pure,
From every ill can good transmute,
    And make its change secure.

If thus we find our gifts in thee,
    Its vaster strength will live
To prove its own integrity
    In what we aim to give;
In sense of duty nobly met,
    In nature nobly plain,
In love of men sublimely set
    In diadems of pain.

In statesmen of heroic mold,
    His country's great high priest,
Whose human heart could still enfold
    All things the great, the least;

THE PRAISE OF LINCOLN

Who proved to earth that simple trust
    Is more than Norman blood;
That he is crowned who can be just,
    The great must first be good!

To love is ever to ascend;
    Oh, let our love, like thine,
The nation's highest good attend,
    And with thy spirit shine!
Thus shall our tribute catch from thee
    Its worthiest, noblest, best,
And one united country see,
    Thy life's divine bequest!

O Gettysburg! Thy living dead
    Speak still across the years,
And by thy voice our hearts are led
    Above all passing fears!
But keep, O hills! one record true,
    And one great captain's name!
Oh, then shall all men look to you
    For nation's deathless fame!

GETTYSBURG ODE

Bayard Taylor

(Dedication of the National Monument)

AFTER the eyes that looked, the lips that spake
Here, from the shadows of impending death,
    Those words of solemn breath,
    What voice may fitly break
The silence doubly hallowed, left by him?
We can but bow the head, with eyes grown dim,
    And, as a Nation's litany, repeat

51

The phrase his martyrdom hath made complete,
Noble as then, but now more sadly sweet:
"Let us, the Living, rather dedicate
Ourselves to the unfinished work, which they
Thus far advanced so nobly on its way,
 And save the periled State!
Let us, upon this field where they, the brave,
Their last full measure of devotion gave,
Highly resolve they have not died in vain!—
That, under God, the Nation's later birth
 Of Freedom, and the people's gain
Of their own Sovereignty, shall never wane
And perish from the circle of the earth!"
From such a perfect text, shall Song aspire
 To light her faded fire,
And into wandering music turn
Its virtue, simple, sorrowful, and stern?
His voice all elegies anticipated;
 For, whatsoe'er the strain,
 We hear that one refrain:
"We consecrate ourselves to them, the Consecrated!"

THE LINCOLN BOULDER

Louis Bradford Couch

(Nyack, New York)

O MIGHTY Boulder, wrought by God's own hand,
Throughout all future ages thou shalt stand
A monument of honor to the brave
Who yielded up their lives, their all, to save
Our glorious country, and to make it free
From bondsmen's tears and lash of slavery.

Securely welded to thy rugged breast,
Through all the coming ages there shall rest
Our Lincoln's tribute to a patriot band,
The noblest ever penned by human hand.

The storms of centuries may lash and beat
Thy granite face and bronze with hail and sleet;
But futile all their fury. In a day
The loyal sun shall melt them all away.

Equal in death our gallant heroes sleep
In Southern trench, home grave, or ocean deep;
Equal in glory, fadeless as the light
The stars send down upon them through the night.
O priceless heritage for us to keep
Our heroes' fame immortal while they sleep!
.   .   .   .

O God, still guide us with thy loving hand,
Keep and protect our glorious Fatherland.

THE CABIN WHERE LINCOLN WAS BORN

Robert Morris

ONLY a cabin, old and poor,
Logs and daubing and creaking door;
A solemn sentinel pointing back
Over a century's beaten track,
To a soul that surmounted poverty's hill,
And cried back to the world, "You can if you will."

From his lofty height of power and fame,
Where honor crowned his humble name,
He looked to the cabin that gave him birth,
As the dearest spot of all the earth.
Though born in a cabin, you still will be lucky
If your life is like Lincoln of old Kentucky.

THE MOTHER OF LINCOLN

Benjamin Davenport House

OUT on the lie of "lowly born!"
   For life has never changed its source
   Since first began its earthly course,
Nor from its giver came with scorn.

And they who put in blood their trust,
   Their pride in silk and linen rolled—
   Who band their narrow brows with gold,
Poor fools, they are but common dust.

For flesh is but a robe that clings
   About and clothes the principle
   Of lives which in its swathing dwell,
And only souls are ever kings.

Ah! mother of as grand a son
   As ever battled in the van
   To prove the brotherhood of man,
Such lives as thine are never done.

Though common ways were ways of thine,
   And all thy walks uncarpeted,
   Thou gav'st to earth a life which led
A race enchained to Freedom's shrine.

From out thy hillside hovel came
   An infant's wail, which proved the key
   Of songs of freedom yet to be
To drown the groans—a nation's shame.

Who gives an imbecile to reign,
   The worn-out stock of royal line—
   Backed by the lie of "right divine"—
Is less than handmaid in thy train.

THE PRAISE OF LINCOLN

We can but wonder, we who read
  The past with backward, searching look,
  Its pages open as a book,
If thou foresaw where he would lead.

If, gazing in the embers' glow,
  Thine eyes by dreaming fancy held,
  Thou saw'st the flames that would unweld
The chains and let the bondsman go?

When baby fingers touched thy breast,
  If ever in thy musing then
  Thou dream'dst that hand should guide the pen
Whose stroke would free a race oppressed?

Didst hear, O mother! when blew free
  The winds which through the crannies sighed,
  The sounds of voices as they cried,
Because the light they could not see?

Or when the north wind's trumpets blew
  Heardst thou in them wild war's alarms?
  The cannon's roar, or clash of arms
Where shot-torn battle banners flew?

Thou wert unstoried and unsung,
  O mother of our mighty dead!
  Of whom thy life was fountain head,
Yet History's harp for thee is strung.

For, from the iron of thy blood
  Was forged the nation-needed life
  Which, when the land was torn with strife,
Stood Freedom's pharos 'midst the flood.

THE PRAISE OF LINCOLN

We can not know, thou lost to earth,
  That ever came a dream to thee
   Of what the nation's fate should be,
Led by the life thou gavest birth;

But trust looks forward with belief
  That thou hast fullest knowledge gained,
   Through larger life thou hast attained,
And hold it as a garnered sheaf.

That thou hast pierced life curtain's mesh
  With all the soul of sense and sound,
   Unhampered by the narrow bound,
Of sight and sound of sense of flesh.

Hast heard the battle sink to rest,
  Succeeded by the thunder roll
   Of welcome to the mighty soul
Whose life was nurtured at thy breast.

THE HOUSE WHERE LINCOLN DIED

Robert Mackay

ABOVE Judea's purple-mantled plain,
  There hovers still, among the ruins lone,
  The spirit of the Christ whose dying moan
Was heard in heaven, and paid our debt in pain.

As subtle perfume lingers with the rose,
  Even when its petals flutter to the earth,
  So clings the potent mystery of the birth
Of that deep love from which all mercy flows.

. . . .

56

THE PRAISE OF LINCOLN

Within this house, this room,—a martyr died,
   A prophet of a larger liberty,—
   A liberator setting bondmen free,
A full-orbed man, above mere mortal pride.

The cloud-rifts opening to celestial glades
   Oft glimpse him, and his spirit lingers still,
   As Christ's sweet influence breathes upon the hill
Where the red lily with the sunset fades.

   .   .   .   .

A little girl, with eyes of heavenly blue,
   Sings through the old place, ignorant of all;
   Her angel face, her cheerful, birdlike call
Thrilling the heart to life more full, more true.

THE NEGLECTED GRAVE OF
LINCOLN'S MOTHER

James Corbin

A WOODED hill—a low-sunk grave
   Upon the hilltop hoary;
The oak tree's branches o'er it wave;
Devoid of slab—no record save
   Tradition's story.

And who the humble dead, that here
   So lonely sleeps?
And who, as year rolls after year,
In summer green or autumn sere—
   Comes here and weeps?

So lone and drear—the forest wild
   Unbroken seems—
We well might think some forest child,
Grown tired of hunt or war trail wild,
   Here lies and dreams.

But no; no red man of the West
   Inhabits here;
These clods so oft by wild beast pressed,
Now lie upon the breast
   Of one more dear.

For Lincoln's mother here is laid—
   Far from her son.
No long procession, false parade
Of pride or place was here displayed—
   No requiem sung.

No summer friends were crowded round
   Her humble grave.
The summer breezes bore no sound,
Save genuine grief, when this lone mound
   Its echoes gave.

Her husband and her children dear,
   And neighbors rude,
Dressed in their hardy homespun gear,
Were all that gathered round her bier,
   In this lone wood.

High pile the marble above the breast
   Of chieftain slain;
While in the wildwood of the West,
In tomb by naught but nature dressed,
   His mother's lain.

Her grave, from art or homage free,
   Neglected lies;
And pomp and pride and vanity,
From this lone grave must ever flee,
   As mockeries.

THE PRAISE OF LINCOLN

'A nation's grief and gratitude
  Bedewed his bier;
For her who sleeps in solitude,
In this lone grave in Western wood,
  Have ye no tear?

And shall the mother of the brave,
  And true and good,
Lie thus neglected in a grave
Unfit for menial, clown or knave
  In this drear wood?

Oh, nation of the generous free,
  Be this your shame;
And let this grave beneath the tree,
No longer thus neglected be,
  Without a name.

ABRAHAM LINCOLN

J. T. Goodman

A NATION lay at rest.   The mighty storm
That threatened their good ship with direful harm,
Had spent its fury; and the tired and worn
Sank in sweet slumber, as the Springtime morn
Dawned with a promise that the strife should cease;
And war's grim face smiled in a dream of peace.
Oh! doubly sweet the sleep when tranquil light
Breaks on the dangers of the fearful night,
And, full of trust, we seek the dreamy realm
Conscious a faithful pilot holds the helm,
Whose steady purpose and untiring hand,
With God's good grace, will bring us safe to land.

THE PRAISE OF LINCOLN

And so the Nation rested, worn and weak
From long exertion—
God! What a shriek
Was that which pierced to farthest earth and sky,
As though all Nature uttered a death cry!
Awake! Arouse! ye sleeping warders, ho!
Be sure this augurs some colossal woe;
Some dire calamity hath passed o'erhead—
A world is shattered or a god is dead!

What! the globe unchanged! The sky still flecked
With stars? Time is? The universe not wrecked?
Then look ye to the pillars of the State!
How fares it with the Nation's good and great?
Since that wild shriek told no unnatural birth
Some mighty Soul has shaken hands with earth.

Lo! murder hath been done. Its purpose foul
Hath stained the marble of the Capitol
Where sat one yesterday without a peer!
Still rests he peerless—but upon his bier.
Ah, faithful heart, so silent now—alack!
And did the Nation fondly call thee back,
And hail thee truest, bravest of the land,
To bare the breast to the assassin's hand?

And yet we know if that extinguished voice
Could be rekindled and pronounce its choice
Between this awful fate of thine, and one—
Retreat from what thou didst or wouldst have done,
In thine own sense of duty, it would choose
This doom—the least a noble soul could lose.

There is a time when the assassin's knife
Kills not, but stabs into eternal life;
And this was such an one. Thy homely name
Was wed to that of Freedom, and thy fame

60

Hung rich and clustering in its lusty prime;
The god of Heroes saw the harvest time,
And smote the noble structure at the root,
That it might bear no less immortal fruit.

Sleep! honored by the Nation and mankind!
Thy name in History's brightest page is shrined,
Adorned by virtues only, and shall exist
Bright and adored on Freedom's martyr list.

The time shall come when on the Alps shall dwell
No memory of their own immortal Tell;
Rome shall forget her Cæsars, and decay
Waste the Eternal City's self away;
And in the lapse of countless ages, Fame
Shall one by one forget each cherished name;
But thine shall live through time, until there be
No soul on earth but glories to be free.

THE MARTYR

Christopher Pearce Cranch

No, NOT in vain he died, not all in vain,—
Our good, great President. This people's hands
Are linked together in one mighty chain,
Knit tighter now in triple woven bands,
To crush the fiends in human mask, whose might
We suffer, oh, too long! The devils we must fight
With fire. God wills it in this deed. This use
We draw from the most impious murder done
Since Calvary. Rise, then, O countrymen!
Scatter the marsh-light hopes of Union won
Through pardoning clemency. Strike, strike again!
Draw closer round the foe a girdling flame!
We are stabbed whene'er we spare. Strike, in God's
    name!

LINCOLN

Benjamin S. Parker

(February 12th, 1809—February 12th, 1909)

LEAN child of the rugged hills,
    Warmed by the auroral flame;
Thine is a hist'ry that fills
    And thrills the loud trump of fame!
Swart wielder of axe and maul,
    Companion of toil and care;
Oh, never at duty's call
    Was a heart more brave to bear—
More tender to pain, more sure
    To hold to the deathless right
And calumny's shafts endure
    For sake of the hoped-for light,
Than thine, O prophet-soul, that held in fee
The truth that is, the greater truth to be.

By the cabin's hearth of clay,
    Bent over the sentient page,
By the wood-fire's fitful ray,
    From the hero and the sage,
Safe into thy inmost thought
    Absorbing the things most wise
By Grecian and Roman taught,
    Men see thee, in humble guise,—
A boy with the morning glow
    Of genius on thy face,—
A light for the world to know
    Through time's far-reaching space—
A light, a torch, a flame of living fire
To lead the way wherever souls aspire.

THE PRAISE OF LINCOLN

Once scoff of the worldly wise
  Who sneered at thy honest fame,
And with anger-flashing eyes
  Announced it the country's shame
That the people thronged to see
  As their chosen leader, friend,
Whose vision was clear to see,
  And who would not break nor bend,
Though the nation's weight of sin
  Should upon thy shoulders fall
Through the gathering wrath and din
  Of Bellona's carnival.
When mummers and maskers should rend the flag,
And tread it in dust, a dishonored rag.

Then, with thy hand on the wheel,
  And the world's hope in thy hand,
With sensitive nerves to feel
  Each throb of pain in the land,
Quick to the sorrowing's cry,
  Yet firm as the basic rock
To the war waves roaring by
  And the battle's awful shock;
What a strong god's task was thine,
  With brother at brother's throat,
To keep through the strength divine,
  The brave ship of state afloat
On the sea of nations, where she alone
Carried Freedom's flag to the breezes thrown.

The flag of liberty, stained
  By blood of the driven thrall
That on every new star gained
  Let its festering shadow fall,

THE PRAISE OF LINCOLN

As a cloud that dripped down gore,
   Polluting the land and sea
And presaging evermore
   The vict'ry of savagery;
Should the freeman hunt the slave,
   As the serf of remorseless ill,
Or the nation find its grave
   Through the loss of its manly will?
Right won the forum, but passion brought
The crush of battle from the clash of thought.

And the wild war thundered on
   And the Union's hope seemed vain,
Till thy hand was laid upon
   The source of that fetid stain:
The strokes of thy prophet pen
   That made the millions free
And cleansed "Old Glory" then,
   For the millions yet to be,
All glowing with fadeless light
   Deep into the darkness hurled
To banish the reign of night
   From the empire of the world,
Appealed to the nobler soul of the race,
And the army moved with a conqu'ror's pace.

In sorrow and not in wrath
   Did thine eyes survey the woe—
War's horrors and aftermath.
   In anguish of friend and foe—
For thou hadst the Master's art
   To bring to the fainting cheer,
To solace the breaking heart,
   Or quiet the captive's fear,

THE PRAISE OF LINCOLN

To free the fond mother's boy
  From a death of ignoble pain;
Turn bitterness into joy
  And defeat into future gain,
And thy opportune humor's gentle play
Was sunshine and cheer for the darkest day.

And then, with the end in sight—
  With the dawn's white glow of peace
Enlarging to fuller light
  With promise of swift increase,
As the war clouds rolled apart—
  Thy thoughts with forgiveness filled
And thy sympathetic heart
  By the fatal shot were stilled,
The people bowed down in tears
  And the night consumed the day,
But yet through the testing years
  Man yields to thy spirit's sway:
Death claimed thee ere all thy work was done,
But thy star was risen, thy glory won.

O Martyr! yet more than King,
  Forgive us our feeble words
And the fading wreaths we bring,
  When voices of free, wild birds,
The breeze and the prairie flowers,
  Bear thee, in thy western tomb,
Love's tributes exceeding ours,—
  Perennials of song and bloom:
Forgive us if we forget,
  When our brooding ills provoke,
The pattern thy patience set,
  Or shackles thy brave hands broke,
But forgive us not if our haughty pride
Has the righteous plea of the weak denied.

God keepeth His universe
    And brings the man and the hour
To strangle each haunting curse
    And banish its evil power,
And each new crisis finds
    Its hero of lofty soul
With the strength of myriad minds
    To lead, to redeem, console;
But, bearers of hope and light,
    No two are alike, nor cast,
From shadows of ancient might,
    In molds of an outgrown past:
Fame knows but one Lincoln—He stands alone—
The boy from the cabin, our loved, our own.

LINCOLN

Wilbur D. Nesbit

WE mark the lowly place where he was born,
    We try to dream the dreams that starred his nights
When the rude path that ran beside the corn
    Grew to a fair broad way that found the heights;
We try to sense the lonely days he knew,
    The silences that wrapped about his soul
When there came whispers tremulous and true
    Which urged him up and onward to his goal.

His was the dream-filled world of kindly trees;
    And marvel-reaches of the prairie lands;
The brotherhood of fields, and birds, and bees,
    Which magnifies the soul that understands;
His was the school of unremitting toil
    Whose lessons leave an impress strong and deep;
His were the thoughts of one close to the soil,
    The knowledge of the ones who sow and reap.

THE PRAISE OF LINCOLN

And of all this, and from all this, he rose
    Full panoplied, when came his country's call,
Strong-hearted, and strong-framed to bear the woes
    Which fell on him the bitterest of all.
And well he wrought, and wisely well he knew
    The strain and stress that should be his alone;
He did the task long set for him to do—
    This man who came unfavored and unknown.

We look to-day, not through Grief's mist of tears,
    Not through glamour of nearness to the great,
But down the long, long corridor of years
    Where stand the sentinels of Fame and Fate,
And now we see him, whom men called uncouth,
    Grown wondrous fair beneath the hand of Time,
And know the love of liberty and truth
    Brings immortality, and makes sublime.

But, oh, this rugged face with kindly eyes
    Wherein a haunting sorrow ever stays!
Somehow it seems that through the sorrow rise
    The echoed visions of his other days,
That still we may in subtle fancy trace
    The light that led him with prophetic gleams—
That here we gaze upon the pictured face
    Of one who was a boy that lived his dreams.

LINCOLN

John E. Barrett

FAME's trumpet blows a silver note
    Across the ebbing sea of time,
And angels on the farther shore
    In rapture chant its song sublime.

THE PRAISE OF LINCOLN

It sings of peace, of broken chains,
  Of cruel wrong at last made right;
Of franchised millions lifted up
  From thraldom into freedom's light.

It tells of manhood's grandest act—
  The liberation of a race
From centuried oppression's grasp
  And grinding greed to power and place.

It links the freedom of the slave,
  Upon whose neck a nation's shame
Was laid through years of tyranny,
  With Lincoln's everlasting name.

TO A PORTRAIT OF ABRAHAM
LINCOLN

Edith Colby Banfield

THY rugged features more heroic are
  Than chiselled outlines of some godlike Greek;
  Thy steadfast lips more eloquent did speak
Than lips of orators renowned afar;
While gentle wit and tolerance of folly,
  And human sympathies and love of right
  Shone never with more kind and steady light
Than from the cavern of thy melancholy.
O prophet sorrowful, did thy deep eyes
Foresee and weep thy country's agonies?
  And did thy lonely heart foreread thy doom
  To give thy brow such majesty of gloom?
Ah, hadst thou seen the end, thou still hadst led
Thy people with the same unswerving tread!

ABRAHAM LINCOLN

Alice Cary

(Foully Assassinated, April, 1865. Inscribed to Punch)

No GLITTERING chaplet brought from other lands!
  As in his life, this man, in death, is ours;
His own loved prairies o'er his "gaunt gnarled hands"
  Have fitly drawn their sheet of summer flowers.

What need hath he now of a tardy crown,
  His name from mocking sneer and jest to save?
When every plowman turns his furrow down
  As soft as though it fell upon his grave.

He was a man whose like the world again
  Shall never see, to vex with blame or praise:
The landmarks that attest his bright, brief reign
  Are battles, not the pomps of gala-days!

The grandest leader of the grandest war
  That ever time in history gave a place;
What were the tinsel flattery of a star
  To such a breast! or what a ribbon's grace!

'Tis to the man, and the man's honest worth,
  The nation's loyalty in tears upsprings;
Through him the soil of labor shines henceforth
  High o'er the silken braideries of kings.

The mechanism of external forms—
  The shifts that courtiers put their bodies through,
Were alien ways to him—his brawny arms
  Had other work than posturing to do!

Born of the people, well he knew to grasp
   The wants and wishes of the weak and small;
Therefore we hold him with no shadow clasp—
   Therefore his name is household to us all.

Therefore we love him with a love apart
   From any fawning love of pedigree—
His was the royal soul and mind and heart—
   Not the poor outward shows of royalty.

Forgive us then, O friends, if we are slow
   To meet your recognition of his worth—
We're jealous of the very tears that flow
   From eyes that never loved a humble hearth.

LINCOLN

S. Weir Mitchell

(Newport, October, 1891)

CHAINED by stern duty to the rock of state,
   His spirit armed in mail of rugged mirth,
   Ever above, though ever near the earth,
Yet felt his heart the vulture beaks that sate
Base appetites, and foul with slander, wait
   Till the keen lightnings bring the awful hour
   When wounds and sufferings shall give them power.
Most was he like to Luther, gay and great,
   Solemn and mirthful, strong of heart and limb.
   Tender and simple too; he was so near
   To all things human that he cast out fear,
And, ever simpler, like a little child,
   Lived in unconscious nearness unto Him
Who always on earth's little ones hath smiled.

OUR GOOD PRESIDENT

Phœbe Cary

Our sun hath gone down at the noon-day,
 The heavens are black;
And over the morning, the shadows
 Of night-time are back.

Stop the proud boasting mouth of the cannon;
 Hush the mirth and the shout;—
God is God! and the ways of Jehovah
 Are past finding out.

Lo! the beautiful feet on the mountains,
 That yesterday stood,
The white feet that came with glad tidings
 Are dabbled in blood.

The Nation that firmly was settling
 The crown on her head,
Sits like Rizpah, in sackcloth and ashes,
 And watches her dead.

Who is dead? who, unmoved by our wailing,
 Is lying so low?
O my Land, stricken dumb in your anguish,
 Do you feel, do you know,

That the hand which reached out of the darkness
 Hath taken the whole;
Yea, the arm and the head of the people,
 The heart and the soul?

And that heart, o'er whose dread awful silence
 A nation has wept;
Was the truest, the gentlest, the sweetest,
 A man ever kept.

THE PRAISE OF LINCOLN

Why, he heard from the dungeons, the rice-fields
    The dark holds of ships,
Every faint, feeble cry which oppression
    Smothered down on men's lips.

In her furnace, the centuries had welded
    Their fetter and chain;
And like withes, in the hands of his purpose,
    He snapped them in twain.

Who can be what he was to the people,—
    What he was to the state?
Shall the ages bring to us another
    As good and as great?

Our hearts with their anguish are broken,
    Our wet eyes are dim;
For us is the loss and the sorrow,
    The triumph for him!

For, ere this, face to face with his Father
    Our martyr hath stood;
Giving into His hand a white record,
    With its great seal of blood.

THE VOICE OF DESTINY

Lyman Whitney Allen

THE hour was come, and in that hour he stood
    Responsive to the sacred voice that spoke
    From Heaven and earth and sea.
He heard the dusky toiling multitude
    Plaintively pleading that his hand should break
    Their bonds and set them free.

He heard the voice of God from shining height,
  Who, for the reason of the Nation's sin,
    Had held her armies back
In failure and defeat, till she should right
  The wrongs herself had sanctioned, and should win
    Justice unto her track;

When, girded with the strength of righteousness,
  God for her, with descending seraphim,
    Above the battle's tide,
She then would march to triumph, and possess
  A land united to the farthest rim,
    Through sorrow purified.

THE MARTYR

Herman Melville

(Indicative of the Passion of the People on the 15th of
April, 1865)

GOOD Friday was the day
  Of the prodigy and crime,
When they killed him in his pity,
  When they killed him in his prime
Of clemency and calm—
  When with yearning he was filled
  To redeem the evil-willed,
And, though conqueror, be kind;
  But they killed him in his kindness,
  In their madness, in their blindness,
And they killed him from behind.

There is sobbing of the strong,
  And a pall upon the land;
But the People in their weeping
  Bare the iron hand:
Beware the People weeping
  When they bare the iron hand.

73

THE PRAISE OF LINCOLN

He lieth in his blood—
　　The father in his face;
They have killed him, the Forgiver—
　　The Avenger takes his place,
The Avenger wisely stern,
　　Who in righteousness shall do
　　What the heavens call him to,
And the parricides remand;
　　For they killed him in his kindness,
　　In their madness and their blindness,
And his blood is on their hand.

　　There is sobbing of the strong,
　　　　And a pall upon the land;
　　But the People in their weeping
　　　　Bare the iron hand:
　　Beware the People weeping
　　　　When they bare the iron hand.

THE DEAR PRESIDENT

John James Piatt

(April 19th, 1865)

ABRAHAM LINCOLN, the Dear President,
Lay in the Round Hall at the Capitol,
And there the people came to look their last.

There came the widow, weeded for her mate;
There came the mother, sorrowing for her son;
There came the orphan, moaning for its sire.

There came the soldier, bearing home his wound;
There came the slave, who felt his broken chain;
There came the mourners of a blackened land.

THE PRAISE OF LINCOLN

Through the dark April day, a ceaseless throng,
They passed the coffin, saw the sleeping face,
And, blessing it, in silence moved away.

And one, a poet, spake within his heart:
"It harmed him not to praise him when alive,
And me it shall not harm to praise him dead.

"Too oft the muse has blushed to speak of men—
No muse shall blush to speak her best of him,
And still to speak her best of him is dumb.

"O lofty wisdom's low simplicity!
O awful tenderness of voted power!—
No man e'er held so much of power so meek.

"He was the husband of the husbandless,
He was the father of the fatherless:
Within his heart he weighed the common woe.

"His call was like a father's to his sons!
As to a father's voice, they, hearing, came—
Eager to offer, strive, endure, and die.

"The mild bond-breaker, servant of the Lord,
He took the sword, but in the name of Peace,
And touched the fetter, and the bound was free.

"Oh, place him not among historic kings,
Strong, barbarous chiefs and bloody conquerors,
But with the great and pure Republicans:

"Those who have been unselfish, wise and good,
Bringers of Light and Pilots in the Dark,
Bearers of Crosses, Servants of the World.

"And always, in his Land of birth and death,
Be his fond name—warmed in the people's hearts—
Abraham Lincoln, the Dear President."

LINCOLN

Benjamin S. Parker

(Indianapolis, April 30th, A. D. 1865)

THE voice is hushed, the heart is still,
  No light is in the earnest eye
That lately looked on war's wild ill
  And wept where fallen heroes lie.

We kindle brightly to thy praise,
  We melt in sorrow at thy bier,
And wonder, in the boundless days,
  When God shall every truth insphere

In worlds all wisdom, all delight,
  What crowns thy spirit brow shall wear,
When past the terror and the night,
  Thou soarest into morning there.

O choral lips of love and song!
  The world's harmonic multitude
That through the ages dim and long,
  Have prophesied the coming good,—

Philosopher and saint and seer,
  Of every age and race and clime,—
Behold the promised days are near,
  Auroral on the hills of time.

We read the blessed morrow's sign,
  That comes to hallow every place,
In every feature, every line
  Of that upturned and calmest face.

THE PRAISE OF LINCOLN

From this dear sacrifice we learn
  That future's full reality,
How freedom's flame shall mount and burn
  Above the tomb of slavery.

How age on age shall pile its weight;
  Yet through the twilight dim and far,
Among the wise and good and great,
  Shall Lincoln shine, a morning star.

The useless lash, the broken chain,
  Black swarms of traffic turn to men,
War fruiting with eternal gain,
  That ripens into peace again.

These glorify the places where
  Thy paths have been, O true and brave!
And these inspire the prairie air
  To sing its rest above thy grave.

Rest! patriot, martyr, savior, friend,
  Defender of the poor and weak!
Thy glory shall not have an end
  While history has a voice to speak.

THE VISION OF ABRAHAM LINCOLN

Wendell Phillips Garrison

(April 14th, 1865)

DREAMING, he woke, our Martyr President,
  And still the vision lingered in his mind,
  (Problem at once and prophecy combined)—
A flying bark with all her canvas bent:

THE PRAISE OF LINCOLN

Joy-bringing herald of some great event
  Oft when the wavering scale of war inclined
  To Freedom's side; now how to be divined
Uncertain, since rebellion's force was spent.
So, of the omen heedful, as of Fate,
  Lincoln with curious eye the horizon scanned:
At morn, with hopes of port and peace elate;
  At night, like Palinurus—in his hand
The broken tiller of the Ship of State—
  Flung on the margin of the Promised Land.

ABRAHAM LINCOLN

James Nicoll Johnston

(Lying in State in Buffalo, April 27th, 1865)

BEAR him to his Western home,
  Whence he came four years ago;
Not beneath some Eastern dome,
But where Freedom's airs may come,
  Where the prairie grasses grow,
  To the friends who loved him so.

Take him to his quiet rest;
  Toll the bell and fire the gun;
He who served his country best,
He whom millions loved and bless'd,
  Now has fame immortal won;
  Rack of brain and heart is done.

Shed thy tears, O April rain!
  O'er the tomb wherein he sleeps!
Wash away the bloody stain!
Drape the skies in grief, O rain!
  Lo! a nation with thee weeps,
  Grieving o'er her martyred slain.

78

THE PRAISE OF LINCOLN

To the people whence he came,
  Bear him gently back again,
Greater his than victor's fame;
His is now a sainted name;
  Never ruler had such gain—
  Never people had such pain.

LINCOLN

Orpheus C. Kerr

(Robert Henry Newell)

I

'Twas needed—the name of a Martyr sublime,
To vindicate God in that terrible time!
'Twas fitting the thunder of Heaven should roll,
Ere cannon exultant had deafened the soul
To what in all ages the Maker had taught,
The pardon of sin is with suffering bought,
And just was the doom that the lightning should fall
On him, the supreme and head of us all,
Ere, blest in his living the triumph to seal,
The Victor forgot what the Brother should feel.
For still with the vanquished we shared in the guilt
That struck us at last to the murderous hilt;
And still unto us did the horror belong
Of helping a brother to wed with the Wrong,
Till fostered to treason by parent and kin,
A traitor to both was the child of the sin.
Then thine to atone for the shame in the end,
Our gentle First Citizen, Chieftain, and Friend.

79

II

And honestly plain as thyself be the verse
Such living and dying as thine to rehearse;
Not tuned to the rhythmical music of art,
But simple of note as the pulse of the heart
That answers the touch of the hand on the strings
When man for the noblest humanity sings.
From page unto page of thy story we trace
The strength of thy manhood, the light of thy face:
Thy merciful soul and thy wisdom are there;
An honesty open and clear as the air;
A spirit to mold from the fetters of birth,
A crown for a peer of the kings of the earth;
A nature to wear in the palace of State
The mind of the humble that stand in the gate;
A grace, of humanity's brotherhood bred,
To bend with the wrong to the lowliest head;
To bear up the height unto Freedom the Slave,
And find upon Pisgah his thanks—and a grave!

III

How pure is the luster of virtues that climb
Imperial summits of power in their time,
Unaided by patronage, conquest, or birth,
But lifted aloft by the magic of worth:
Like jewels in primal reflection that shine,—
Not drawn from a casket, but raised from the mine,
A growth from the sunless domain of the moles,
Yet born with a splendor of light in their souls!
Behold where the boy at the plow in the West
Inherits such virtues to glow in his breast:
He knows not his riches; he bends to his toil,
Where scant is the harvest and stubborn the soil;
While broods in his bosom such patience serene
As giveth to labor its tenderest mien.

THE PRAISE OF LINCOLN

None tell to the liegeless of houses and lands
The fate of a people shall rest in his hands;
Yet sleeps there a might in the calm of his eye
To rescue a nation from death—and to die!

IV

Oh, bitterest lot that the lowly can find,
Where labor's monotony crushes the mind,
Till poverty, prisoned in poverty still,
To dust is degraded, or maddened to kill.
'Tis thus in the countries far over the sea,
But happy the poor man, my Country, in thee;
For wide over thee may his industry range,
And sweeten his toil with the blessing of change.
From tracing the furrow and planting the grain,
The youth turneth back and forsaketh the plain:
He mates with the boatmen, and joins in their song,
Where rolleth the Father of Waters along:
Still patient with fortune, still earnest to bear
What God and humanity mark for his share.
None read from the future his glorious fate,
To stand at the helm of the vessel of State,
Its stay till the night and the tempest are done,
And then into Heaven go up with the sun!

V

Well tried is the genius that rises to rule
From lessons of man in adversity's school:
Ill-balanced by honors too lavishly flung,
It scorneth the level from which it hath sprung;
Imbittered with contest with rank as it rose,
Its texture is iron that hardens with blows;
Or, true to the balance, in victory mild,
It tow'rs like a mountain grown up from the wild;

THE PRAISE OF LINCOLN

Broad-set at its base in the primitive clod,
To shrink to a spire of the temple of God.
So he, in a grander simplicity hale,
Goes up to a height from obscurity's vale;
So, true to the lowly, sublime to the high,
To these he lends counsel, with those in his eye:
"Half Free and half Slave the Republic must fall;
Yet saved it shall be," are his words for us all!
Time put him to proof when the issue was tried—
He lived for the Deed, for the Principle died!

VI

Now, borne on his countrymen's louder acclaim,
He mounts to the station most noble of fame;
A chief in the halls where a Washington stood,
And like unto him as the good to the good;
Foul Treason has risen, its horrors flame forth
To rouse from their slumbers the souls of the North,
And pealeth from cities, from prairies and farms,
The rallying cry of the loyal in arms.
War breaks on the Nation, she enters the strife
And struggles with traitors for Honor and Life!
Where dwelleth the spirit her being to save
From murderers bred in the toil of the slave?
The Capitol answers: the spirit is there,
And holdeth its court in the President's chair.
That nature so gentle containeth a will
Which glows like a fire in an air that is still—
Alas! that our pillar of guidance by night
Should fade from the world at the coming of light!

VII

Why follow the record? His glories are told
In all that the people the tenderest hold:
A nation redeemed, and her banner unfurled
The fairest, the strongest, the best in the world.

THE PRAISE OF LINCOLN

Henceforth be that banner to patriot eyes
A prayer from its Shepherd of Stars in the skies,—
To plead that no judgment in malice may fall,
To speak for a charity free unto all,
To glow on the sword that is drawn for the Right,
While merciful still in the midst of the fight:
Henceforth be its legend for ages to view,
Its stripes of the dawn and its planeted blue,
That ere from its story the darkness was torn,
A something of Heaven shed blood on the morn,
In sign that 'tis given the godlike of earth
To pass through a death for the millions' new birth,—
To die of the night's weary vigil and care,
When day the eternal first whitens the air.

LINCOLN'S LAST DREAM

Hezekiah Butterworth

I

APRIL flowers were in the hollows; in the air were
     April bells,
And the wings of purple swallows rested on the battle
     shells.
From the war's long scene of horror now the nation
     found release;
All the day the old war bugles blew the blessed note of
     peace.
     'Thwart the twilight's damask curtains
          Fell the night upon the land,
     Like God's smile of benediction
          Shadowed faintly by his hand.
In the twilight, in the dusklight, in the starlight, every-
     where,
Banners waved like garden flowers in the palpitating
     air.

II

In Art's temple there were greetings, gentle hurryings
of feet,
And triumphant strains of music rose amid the num-
bers sweet,
Soldiers gathered, heroes gathered, women beautiful
were there:
Will *he* come, the man Beloved, there to rest an hour
from care?
 Will he come who for the people
  Long the cross of pain has borne,—
 Prayed in silence, wept in silence,
  Held the hand of God alone?
Will he share the hour of triumph, now his mighty
work is done?
Here receive the people's plaudits, now the victory is
won?

III

O'er thy dimpled waves, Potomac, softly now the
moonbeams creep;
O'er fair Arlington's green meadows, where the brave
forever sleep,
'Tis Good Friday; bells are tolling, bells of chapel beat
the air
On thy quiet shores, Potomac; Arlington, serene and
fair.
 And he comes, the nation's hero,
  From the White House, worn with care;
 Hears the name of "Lincoln!" ringing
  In the thronged streets everywhere;
Hears the bells,—what memories bringing to his long-
uplifted heart!
Hears the plaudits of the people as he gains the Hall of
Art.

IV

Throbs the air with thrilling music, gayly onward
    sweeps the play;
But he little heeds the laughter, for his thoughts are
    far away;
And he whispers faintly, sadly, "Oft a blessed Form I
    see,
Walking calmly 'mid the people on the shores of Gali-
    lee;
    Oft I've wished His steps to follow,
      Follow Him, the Man Divine;
    When the cares of state are over,
      I will go to Palestine,
And the paths the Blessed followed I will walk from
    sea to sea,
Follow Him who healed the people on the shores of
    Galilee."

V

Hung the flag triumphant o'er him; and his eyes with
    tears were dim,
Though a thousand eyes before him lifted oft their
    smiles to him.
Forms of statesmen, forms of heroes, women beautiful
    were there,
But it was another vision that had calmed his brow of
    care:
    Tabor glowed in light before him,
      Carmel in the evening sun;
    Faith's strong armies grandly marching
      Through the vale of Esdralon:
Bethany's palm-shaded gardens, where the Lord the
    sisters met,
And the Pascal moon arising o'er the brow of Olivet.

VI

Now the breath of light applauses rose the templed
    arches through,
Stirred the folds of silken banners, mingled red and
    white and blue;
But the Dreamer seemed to heed not: rose the past his
    eyes before,—
Armies guarding the Potomac, flashing through the
    Shenandoah;
    Gathering armies, darkening navies,
      Heroes marching forth to die;
    Chickamauga, Chattanooga,
      And the Battle of the Sky;
Silent prayers to free the bondmen in the ordeal of fire,
And God's angel's sword uplifted to fulfill his heart's
    desire.

VII

Thought he of the streets of Richmond on the late
    triumphant day
When the swords of vanquished leaders at his feet sur-
    rendered lay;
When, amid the sweet bells ringing, all the sabled
    multitudes
Shouted forth the name of "Lincoln!" like a rushing
    of the floods;
    Thought of all his heart had suffered;
      All his struggles and renown;
    Dreaming not that just above him
      Lifted was the martyr's crown;
Seeing not the dark form stealing through the music-
    haunted air;
Knowing not that 'mid the triumph the betrayer's feet
    were there.

86

THE PRAISE OF LINCOLN

VIII

Flash! what scymetar of fire lit the flag with lurid
      light?
Hush! what means the shuddering silence, what that
      woman's shriek of fright?
Puff of smoke? the call-bell ringing? why has stopped
      the airy play?
Why the fixed looks of the players that a moment past
      were gay?
    Why the murmurings, strange, uncertain,
    Why do faces turn so white,
    Why descends the affrighted curtain
    Like a wild cloud 'thwart the sight?
Why the brute cries? why the tumult? Has Death
      found the Hall of Art?
Hush! What say those quivering whispers turning
      into stone each heart?

IX

April morning; flags are blowing; 'thwart each flag a
      sable bar.
Dead the leader of the people; dead, the world's great
      commoner.
Bells on the Potomac tolling; tolling by the Sangamon;
Tolling from the broad Atlantic to the Ocean of the
      Sun.
    Friend and foe clasp hands in silence,
    Listen to the low prayers said,
    Hear the people's benedictions,
    Hear the nations praise the dead.
Lovely land of Palestine! he thy shores shall never see,
But, his dream fulfilled, he follows Him who walked in
      Galilee.

LINCOLN'S PASSING BELL

Lucy Larcom

(April 15th, 1865)

TOLLING, tolling, tolling!
  All the bells of the land!
Lo! the patriot martyr
  Taketh his journey grand;
Travels into the ages,
  Bearing a hope how dear!
Into life's unknown vistas,
  Liberty's great pioneer.

Tolling, tolling, tolling!
  Do the budded violets know
The pain of the lingering clangor
  Shaking their bloom out so?
They open into strange sorrow,
  The rain of a nation's tears;
Into the saddest April
  Twined with the New World's years.

Tolling, tolling, tolling!
  See, they come as a cloud,—
Hearts of a mighty people,
  Bearing his pall and shroud!
Lifting up, like a banner,
  Signals of loss and woe!
Wonder of breathless nations,
  Moveth the solemn show.

Tolling, tolling, tolling!
  Was it, O man beloved,—
Was it thy funeral only,
  Over the land that moved?

Veiled by that hour of anguish,
  Borne with the rebel rout,
Forth into utter darkness,
  Slavery's corse went out.

FOR THE SERVICES IN MEMORY
OF ABRAHAM LINCOLN

Oliver Wendell Holmes

(City of Boston, June 1st, 1865—Choral: Luther's
  "Judgment Hymn")

O THOU of soul and sense and breath,
  The ever-present Giver,
Unto thy mighty Angel, Death,
  All flesh thou dost deliver;
What most we cherish we resign,
For life and death alike are thine,
  Who reignest Lord forever!

Our hearts lie buried in the dust
  With him so true and tender,
The patriot's stay, the people's trust,
  The shield of the offender;
Yet every murmuring voice is still,
As, bowing to thy sovereign will,
  Our best-loved we surrender.

Dear Lord, with pitying eye behold
  This martyr generation,
Which thou, through trials manifold,
  Art showing thy salvation!
O let the blood by murder spilt
Wash out thy stricken children's guilt
  And sanctify our nation!

THE PRAISE OF LINCOLN

Be thou thy orphaned Israel's friend,
  Forsake thy people never,
In One our Broken Many blend,
  That none again may sever!
Hear us, O Father, while we raise
With trembling lips our song of praise,
  And bless thy name forever!

ABRAHAM LINCOLN

Amasa Stetson Condon

COLUMBIA'S PROPHECY, FEBRUARY 12TH, 1809

SOMEWHERE to-day in dolor and in want,
  Where tears are plenty and bread is scarce,
And prowling ghosts from a luckless haunt
  Make home a mockery and life a farce;
Like the dissonant wail from a tuneless chord,
There the first low wail of a child shall be heard.

And the large asking eyes full of baby awe,
  That will question the cheer of the wretched den,
Shall behold, rising out of this cradle of straw,
  A temple ornate with affections of men;
And when my bright stars shall be paling their hue,
Then his hand shall recast the whole field of blue.

THE FULFILMENT, APRIL 14, 1865

Let cunning lips that are crafty in speech,
  Praise "My Royal Lord" and his Lady proud;
Let pliant tongues loquacious preach
  Of the baron bold and his noble blood;
Let knights call the names of their fathers up,
  And toast them with jeweled lance in rest,
But with humble hand I will raise a cup
  To one that is greater than their guest.

90

THE PRAISE OF LINCOLN

We will pour from a lip in the tangled horn,
    A milk-white draught that the Crete adored,
To celebrate a patriot born
    In a tree-nailed box of rough deal board;
We will drink to him whose infant eyes
    Looked first on clouds of a leaden hue,
That hanging dense in the morning skies,
    Hid the Orient beams of the sun from view.

Till the climax that finished a glorified life,
    These furrowing sorrows he patiently bore;
And the long, painful years of a crucial strife
    Scarce added a line to the horologue's score;
Like a tell-tale map were his lineaments cast,
    In a mold where sufferings had graved their trace;
And always pursuing, this ghost of the past
    Told the story pathetic on his face.

But the boy crept out of poverty's bed,
    To follow the sibyl's magic wand;
And always thereafter, where duty led,
    They journeyed together, hand in hand;
Thou canst trace the stars in the ebon night,
    As they answer the beck of some hidden force;
But how little thou know'st of the subtle might
    That drives them along in their silent course.

So the playful sprite weaves a silken net,
    But its meshes are strong as a web of steel;
At a turn in the path the snare is set
    Where no vigilant eye can its presence reveal;
A captive thenceforth in the fairy train,
    Where censure condemns or glad salvos ring;
But ever he follows the tractile chain,
    A beggar to-day, but to-morrow—a king.

THE PRAISE OF LINCOLN

The hills that grew brown in the bitter breath
　That sifted through clouds the winged snow,
Will sprinkle with blossoms this realm of death,
　When the south wind coaxes the buds to blow;
So genius, if fettered, will languish in gloom,
　Till a herald proclaims the appointed day;
Then 'twill burst the strong door of its sullen tomb,
　If some angel but roll the stone away.

But the tide of events flows white from the shore,
　To bear him away on its stormy breast;
O proud Illinois, he is thine no more!
　He belongs to the world as thy sacred bequest;
There's the altar prepared for this gift of thy love,
　And the fire, and the dirge, and the buffeting throng;
But only the Father in Heaven above
　Can fathom the bounty to outrage and wrong.

But the time is at hand when this man will be tried,
　As gold in a furnace that's heated seven-fold;
If the metal be base we will cast it aside,
　But fire shall determine which is dross, which is
　　gold;
Let the cynic behold, for the trial begins,
　And the test is of wisdom and courage combined;
If his arm be of reed he will fail; if he wins,
　He's the stuff that makes gods of mankind.

On the tempest-torn main, in the offing out yonder,
　The waves clasp the sky and sink down with a roar,
And rolling together with tumult and thunder,
　Break white o'er the sea-wall that circles the shore;
Like the wing of a bird on a faint rim of sky,
　Or the shadow of hope we see in a dream,
The proud Ship of State shakes her canvas on high,
　Defying the storm and the lightning's red gleam.

THE PRAISE OF LINCOLN

But pirates have shifted the buoys from the bar
    To the land-girted harbor, as signals of woe;
And pirates are coaxing where th' gray breakers are,
    And the ship has a deck-load of pirates below;
But the Lincoln that slept in a cradle of straw,
    Stood brave on the bridge with trumpet in hand;
And, peering through darkness and tempest, he saw
    The only safe roadstead that led to the land.

    .   .   .   .

But away with these symbols that baffle my muse,
    And tangle the gait of a smooth-flowing song;
So to happy-eyed Metaphor waving a truce,
    On sturdy Pegasus I'll gallop along.

    .   .   .   .

At a snug little farm-house that stands on a hill,
    A widow grief-stricken bequeathes her last son;
And a fair girl will wait at the tryst by the mill,
    Whose white lips will whisper "Good-bye;" and he's
        gone.
So the villager's hope and the rich city's pride,
    With music that chases the echoes afar,
Float down the broad streets in a living tide,
    To join in the glory and murder of war.

How graphic the picture that drops from a pen
    While a-painting of scenes from those long years of
        dread,
From the fear in the souls of the children of men,
    As they read the long lists of sacrificed dead;—
From the dews of the South turned to red showers of
        rain
    That guttered the turf on the rolling lea,—
From the crimson-lipped bud on the conscious plain,—
    From the grave where Death held his wild jubilee!

THE PRAISE OF LINCOLN

In yon pretty cottage contentment once reigned,
    And all the bright dreams that thrift could inspire,
Now a prey in the grasp of demons unchained,
    And melting away in the hot tongues of fire;
The playground once sacred to childhood's retreat,
    With its carpet of green that lay soft on the earth,
Now trod to a mire by vandal-shod feet,
    And still as the grave are the voices of mirth.

There's the far-reaching lawn; in the arbor below
    Was the rope-braided gig that swept close by the
        spring;
But the leaves have grown black in the path of the foe,
    And a halter is made of the children's swing;
The slow-throbbing drum, and the fife's wailing cry,
    And the voice of a wretch in his brief epilogue,
Proclaim the last act in the fate of a spy,
    Who faces the doom of a dishonored dog.

There the smooth-flowing sea has extinguished its
    foam,
    And soft on its bosom the night tapers burn;
While the sailor-boy dreams of his sweetheart and
    home,
    And the friends of his youth that await his return;
But a black skulking shadow through darkness less
    black,
    Like a fire-breathing courser, plows over the main;
And swift as a sleuth-hound that is hot on the track,
    Submerges its prey in a white-foaming grave.

And thus through the years burned the passions of
    hate,
    As if Satan's new reign on the earth had begun;
Inciting to murder the filial ingrate,
    And guiding the knife to the throat of the son;

THE PRAISE OF LINCOLN

Braiding haloes of flame from a blistered sky,
   Whose fires put to shame the mad rocket's light;
And the iron messengers screaming by
   To gash the red earth in their random flight.

But true to his trust, and with "Right" for his guide,
   'Mid contention at home and confusion abroad,
He held on his way till the foe's humbled pride
   Had thrown down the altars set up to their god;
But how oft, when his own heart was bursting with
     care,
   Did he pause an encouraging word to bestow;—
To patiently heed a supplicant's prayer,
   And speak peace to a mind distracted with woe.

But peace spread her wings to the gaze of the world,
   And the stars sang again in the angels' employ;
While the turbulent banners of discord were furled,
   And the laughing sky rocked with hosannas of joy.
When the battlefield buzzards had stilled their hoarse
     cry,
   And the spirit of hate had fettered its rage;
Then a blow struck him down like a bolt from the sky!
   O God, could I cancel this blot from my page!

But the record is made, and the world knows the
     rest:—
   How it smothered in flowers the grief on his bier;
And mourned him, of men the truest and best,
   That had lived out the span of a mortal's career;
Yes, the record is made, and this man has been tried
   As gold in a furnace that's heated seven-fold;
But the urn holds no dross to throw idly aside,
   For fire hath determined the whole mass is gold.

LINCOLN

B. F. M. Sours

OVER snowy fields of cotton,
  Bend the faces brown and eager;
Over snowy fields of cotton
  Bend the forms with raiment meager.
Theirs the labor, theirs the sunshine,
  Theirs the lash and curse and sorrow;
Theirs the pleading prayers to Heaven
  For some happier to-morrow;
Theirs the suffering of the years,
And the woe and bitter tears.

On all fields of strain and struggle
  Was the black man ever toiling;
On all wide plantation stretches
  Was his freeborn soul recoiling.
There were masters kind and gentle,
  There were masters with their lashes—
See! the age adown the gorges
  Of the wild range madly dashes!
Whither? Whither? Ah! which way?
Earth shall know thy judgment day!

On the block were little babies
  Sold from mothers' warm embraces;
On the block were sold to demons
  Gentle lives with girlish graces;
On the block were husbands, praying,
  Rent from wives all weeping, pleading,
Shrieking in their dread undoing,
  With no strong one interceding—
Crime! crime trod that horrid path
'Neath the God of holy wrath.

96

THE PRAISE OF LINCOLN

Dark—all dark! O for the breaking
  Of the damp, dark night all dreary!
Where is rest, is rest and rapture
  For the sorrowful and weary?
See! the first faint streaks of dawning
  Seem to make the cold sky shiver—
There! athwart the eastern meadows
  Do the red streaks blend and quiver!
Does there dawn a brighter day?
The glad morn is on its way.

Nightmare? Yes; unrest and tossing
  Seemed to shake the nation's slumber;
There were specters and hobgoblins,
  There were ghosts which baffled number.
Old John Brown cast long his shadow
  In the lurid lightning flashes;
Many another seemed to startle;
  Then the dreamer, ghost-mad, dashes,
For the bad, and for the good,
To bathe brother swords in blood.

For a meteor flashed across the sky,
  And it filled the world with dread;
And the flash and the clash of brothers' swords
  Piled field on field with dead:
For God had bathed his sword in Heaven
  To lay a demon low,
To drive a nation to its knees—
  Stubborn—by blow on blow!
And a meteor flashed across the sky
That the inhuman thing might die.

Lincoln! Lincoln! born to scatter
  Shackles from the human cattle—
Born to throne the human instincts
  High above the sullen battle

For the purse and pride and pleasure
    Of a master—born to woo him
For his diadem of glory,
    Bringing joy and manhood to him—
There are millions of men free
Who have not forgotten thee!

For the broken shaft was noble
    Though a foeman did it sever;
And the glory of thee, chieftain,
    Will be sung by bards forever:
For 'twas God above who sent thee
    To the black man who was praying,
To deliver from his bondage,
    And to cease a nation's straying;
And he wrought the work by thee,
That thy fellow-man is free.

ABRAHAM LINCOLN

Monroe Sprowl

In cabined solitude, beside dim fires at midnight hour,
While others drowsed and dreamt of Fame's applause,
This man-to-be carved out his greatfulness,
With purpose stern and true as Pleiades.
He lit a wondrous light in darkened ways,
And set all hearts to song with music sweet,
As when soft, summer rain within the wood
Sets tender leaves to whispering. Grand Lincoln
    heart—
Great Alcyone of men, about whom turns
The universe of Brotherhood. They thought thee poor
And lonely there amid the knotted rails and granite
    hills,

98

THE PRAISE OF LINCOLN

When lo, the skies were thine, and bright Altair
Thy guiding star! The sad heart-cry
For liberty thou heardst amid the din
Of greed and usury, and all thy soul bore down
Unto the charge, as when at Heaven's gate
Great Michael thrust old Satan forth.
At war's Red Sea thy people stood aghast,
And hearts ebbed low in face of that wild flood,
'Til thy uplifted hand of crystal faith
Prevailed with God who guides the Polar sun.
And lo, in awed retreat the cannoned ranks
Fell 'way, and o'er the wreckage shone a path sublime
That led to Peace and happy Freedom's land.
No greater human heart e'er beat in human cause,
Than thine, beloved Lincoln, whom we sing,
As morning stars arise upon the clime
Thy fair love hath embraced. We hear thee call
From sinless heights, and pray God we may go
As sunward ever as thy feet have gone.

WE ARE COMING, FATHER ABRAHAM

James Sloane Gibbons

WE are coming, Father Abraham, three hundred
thousand more,
From Mississippi's winding stream and from New
England's shore;
We leave our plows and workshops, our wives and
children dear,
With hearts too full for utterance and but a silent tear,
We dare not look behind us, but steadily before.
We are coming, Father Abraham, three hundred thou-
sand more.

We are coming, coming, coming; we are coming,
        coming, coming;
We are coming, Father Abraham, three hundred
        thousand more.

If you look across the hill-tops that meet our Northern
        sky,
Long moving lines of rising dust your vision may
        descry;
And now the wind an instant tears the cloudy veil
        aside,
And floats aloft our spangled flag in glory and in pride,
And bayonets in the sunlight gleam and bands brave
        music pour—
We are coming, Father Abraham, three hundred thou-
        sand more.
    We are coming, coming, coming; we are coming,
        coming, coming;
    We are coming, Father Abraham, three hundred
        thousand more.

If you look all down our valleys, where the growing
        harvests shine,
You may see our sturdy farmer boys fast falling into
        line,
And children at their mothers' knees are pulling at the
        weeds,
And learning how to reap and sow against their coun-
        try's needs,
And a farewell group stands weeping at every cottage
        door—
We are coming, Father Abraham, three hundred thou-
        sand more.
    We are coming, coming, coming; we are coming,
        coming, coming;
    We are coming, Father Abraham, three hundred
        thousand more.

You have called us and we're coming by Richmond's
    bloody tide,
To lay us down for Freedom's sake our brothers' bones
    beside,
Or from foul treason's savage grasp to wrench the
    murderous blade,
And in the face of foreign foes its fragments to pa-
    rade;
Six hundred thousand loyal men and true have gone
    before—
We are coming, Father Abraham, three hundred thou-
    sand more.
    We are coming, coming, coming; we are coming,
        coming, coming;
    We are coming, Father Abraham, three hundred
        thousand more.

SONNET IN 1862

John James Piatt

STERN be the Pilot in the dreadful hour
    When a great nation, like a ship at sea
    With the wroth breakers whitening at her lee,
Feels her last shudder if the Helmsman cower;
A godlike manhood be his mighty dower!
    Such and so gifted, Lincoln, may'st thou be
    With thy high wisdom's low simplicity
And awful tenderness of voted power:
From our hot records then thy name shall stand
    On Time's calm ledger out of passionate days—
With the pure debt of gratitude begun,
    And only paid in never-ending praise—
One of the many of a mighty Land,
Made by God's providence the Anointed One.

AN HORATIAN ODE

Richard Henry Stoddard

Not as when some great captain falls
In battle, where his country calls,
   Beyond the struggling lines
   That push his dread designs.

To doom, by some stray ball struck dead:
Or in the last charge, at the head
   Of his determined men,
   Who must be victors then!

Nor as when sink the civic great,
The safer pillars of the State,
   Whose calm, mature, wise words
   Suppress the need of swords!—

With no such tears as e'er were shed
Above the noblest of our dead
   Do we to-day deplore
   The man that is no more!

Our sorrow hath a wider scope,
Too strange for fear, too vast for hope,—
   A wonder, blind and dumb,
   That waits—what is to come!

Not more astonished had we been
If madness, that dark night, unseen
   Had in our chambers crept,
   And murdered while we slept!

THE PRAISE OF LINCOLN

We woke to find a mourning earth—
Our Lares shivered on the hearth,—
   To roof-tree fallen,—all
   That could affright, appall!

Such thunderbolts, in other lands,
Have smitten the rod from royal hands,
   But spared, with us, till now
   Each laureled Cæsar's brow!

No Cæsar he, whom we lament,
A man without a precedent,
   Sent it would seem, to do
   His work—and perish too!

Not by the weary cares of state,
The endless tasks, which will not wait,
   Which, often done in vain,
   Must yet be done again:

Not in the dark wild tide of war,
Which rose so high, and rolled so far,
   Sweeping from sea to sea
   In awful anarchy:—

Four fateful years of mortal strife,
Which slowly drained the nation's life,
   (Yet for each drop that ran
   There sprang an armed man!)

Not then;—but when by measures meet,—
By victory, and by defeat,—
   By courage, patience, skill,
   The people's fixed "We will!"

Had pierced, had crushed rebellion dead,—
Without a hand, without a head:—
    At last, when all was well,
    He fell—O, how he fell!

The time,—the place,—the stealing shape,—
The coward shot,—the swift escape,—
    The wife,—the widow's scream,—
    It is a hideous dream!

A dream?—what means this pageant then?
These multitudes of solemn men,
    Who speak not when they meet,
    But throng the silent street?

The flags half-mast, that late so high
Flaunted at each new victory?
    (The stars no brightness shed,
    But bloody looks the red!)

The cannon's sudden, sullen boom,—
The bells that toll of death and doom,—
    The rolling of the drums,—
    The dreadful car that comes?

Cursed be the hand that fired the shot!
The frenzied brain that hatched the plot!
    Thy country's father slain
    By thee, thou worse than Cain!

Tyrants have fallen by such as thou,
And good hath followed—may it now!
    (God lets bad instruments
    Produce the best events.)

But he, the man we mourn to-day,
No tyrant was: so mild a sway
　In one such weight who bore
　Was never known before!

Cool should he be, of balanced powers,
The ruler of a race like ours,
　Impatient, headstrong, wild,—
　The man to guide the child!

And this he was, who most unfit
(So hard the sense of God to hit!)
　Did seem to fill his place.
　With such a homely face,—

Such rustic manners,—speech uncouth,—
(That somehow blundered out the truth!)
　Untried, untrained to bear
　The more than kingly care!

Ay! And his genius put to scorn
The proudest in the purple born,
　Whose wisdom never grew
　To what, untaught, he knew—

The people, of whom he was one.
No gentleman like Washington,—
　(Whose bones, methinks, make room,
　To have him in their tomb!)

A laboring man, with horny hands,
Who swung the axe, who tilled the lands,
　Who shrank from nothing new,
　But did as poor men do!

THE PRAISE OF LINCOLN

One of the people! Born to be
Their curious epitome;
  To share, yet rise above
  Their shifting hate and love.

Common his mind (it seemed so then),
His thoughts the thoughts of other men:
  Plain were his words, and poor—
  But now they will endure!

No hasty fool, of stubborn will,
But prudent, cautious, pliant, still;
  Who, since his work was good,
  Would do it, as he could.

Doubting, was not ashamed to doubt,
And, lacking prescience, went without:
  Often appeared to halt,
  And was, of course, at fault:

Heard all opinions, nothing loth,
And loving both sides, angered both:
  Was—not like justice, blind,
  But watchful, clement, kind.

No hero, this, of Roman mold;
Nor like our stately sires of old:
  Perhaps he was not great—
  But he preserved the State!

O honest face, which all men knew!
O tender heart, but known to few!
  O wonder of the age,
  Cut off by tragic rage!

THE PRAISE OF LINCOLN

Peace! Let the long procession come,
For hark!—the mournful, muffled drum—
   The trumpet's wail afar,—
   And see! the awful car!

Peace! Let the sad procession go,
While cannon boom, and bells toll slow:
   And go, thou sacred car,
   Bearing our woe afar!

Go, darkly borne, from State to State,
Whose loyal, sorrowing cities wait
   To honor all they can
   The dust of that good man!

Go, grandly borne, with such a train
As greatest kings might die to gain:
   The just, the wise, the brave
   Attend thee to the grave!

And you, the soldiers of our wars,
Bronzed veterans, grim with noble scars,
   Salute him once again,
   Your late commander—slain!

Yes, let your tears, indignant, fall,
But leave your muskets on the wall:
   Your country needs you now
   Beside the forge, the plow!

(When justice shall unsheathe her brand,—
If mercy may not stay her hand,
   Nor would we have it so—
   She must direct the blow!)

And you, amid the master-race,
Who seem so strangely out of place,
　　Know ye who cometh? He
　　Who hath declared ye free!

Bow while the body passes—nay,
Fall on your knees, and weep, and pray!
　　Weep, weep—I would ye might—
　　Your poor, black faces white!

And children, you must come in bands,
With garlands in your little hands,
　　Of blue, and white, and red,
　　To strew before the dead!

So sweetly, sadly, sternly goes
The fallen to his last repose:
　　Beneath no mighty dome,
　　But in his modest home;

The churchyard where his children rest,
The quiet spot that suits him best:
　　There shall his grave be made,
　　And there his bones be laid!

And there his countrymen shall come,
With memory proud, with pity dumb,
　　And strangers far and near,
　　For many and many a year!

For many a year, and many an age,
While history on her ample page
　　The virtues shall enroll
　　Of that paternal soul!

FROM "OUR HEROIC THEMES"

George Henry Boker

CROWN we our heroes with a holier wreath
Than man e'er wore upon this side of death;
Mix with their laurels deathless asphodels,
And chime their peans from the sacred bells!
Nor in your prayers forget the martyred Chief,
Fallen for the gospel of your own belief,
Who, ere he mounted to the people's throne,
Asked for your prayers, and joined in them his own.
I knew the man. I see him, as he stands
With gifts of mercy in his outstretched hands;
A kindly light within his gentle eyes,
Sad as the toil in which his heart grew wise;
His lips half-parted with the constant smile
That kindled truth, but foiled the deepest guile;
His head bent forward, and his willing ear
Divinely patient right and wrong to hear:
Great in his goodness, humble in his state,
Firm in his purpose, yet not passionate,
He led his people with a tender hand,
And won by love a sway beyond command,
Summoned by lot to mitigate a time
Frenzied with rage, unscrupulous with crime,
He bore his mission with so meek a heart
That Heaven itself took up his people's part;
And when he faltered, helped him ere he fell,
Eking his efforts out by miracle.
No king this man, by grace of God's intent;
No, something better, freeman,—President!
A nature, molded, modeled on a higher plan,
Lord of himself, an inborn gentleman!

WHEN LILACS LAST IN THE DOORYARD BLOOMED

Walt Whitman

I

WHEN lilacs last in the dooryard bloomed,
And the great star early drooped in the western sky in
the night,
I mourned, and yet shall mourn with ever-returning
spring.

Ever-returning spring, trinity sure to me you bring,
Lilac blooming perennial and drooping star in the west,
And thought of him I love.

II

O powerful western fallen star!
O shades of night—O moody, tearful night!
O great star disappeared—O the black murk that
hides the star!
O cruel hands that hold me powerless—O helpless
soul of me!
O harsh surrounding cloud that will not free my soul.

III

In the dooryard fronting an old farm-house near the
white-washed palings,
Stands the lilac-bush tall-growing with the heart-
shaped leaves of rich green,
With many a pointed blossom rising delicate, with the
perfume strong I love,

With every leaf a miracle—and from this bush in the
    dooryard,
With delicate-colored blossoms and heart-shaped leaves
    of rich green,
A sprig with its flower I break.

IV

In the swamp in secluded recesses,
A shy and hidden bird is warbling a song.
Solitary the thrush,
The hermit withdrawn to himself, avoiding the settle-
    ments,
Sings by himself a song.

Song of the bleeding throat,
Death's outlet song of life (for well, dear brother, I
    know,
If thou wast not granted to sing thou would'st surely
    die).

V

Over the breast of the spring, the land, amid cities,
Amid lanes and through old woods, where lately the
    violets peeped from the ground, spotting the
    gray debris,
Amid the grass in the fields each side of the lanes,
    passing the endless grass,
Passing the yellow-speared wheat, every grain from its
    shroud in the dark-brown fields uprisen,
Passing the apple-tree blows of white and pink in the
    orchards,
Carrying a corpse to where it shall rest in the grave,
Night and day journeys a coffin.

THE PRAISE OF LINCOLN

VI

Coffin that passes through lanes and streets,
Through day and night with the great cloud darkening
      the land,
With the pomp of the inlooped flags with the cities
      draped in black,
With the show of the States themselves as of crape-
      veiled women standing,
With processions long and winding and the flambeaus
      of the night,
With the countless torches lit, with the silent sea of
      faces and the unbared heads,
With the waiting depot, the arriving coffin, and the
      somber faces,
With the dirges through the night, with the thousand
      voices rising strong and solemn,
With all the mournful voices of the dirges poured
      around the coffin,
The dim-lit churches and the shuddering organs—
      where amid these you journey,
With the tolling, tolling bell's perpetual clang,
Here, coffin that slowly passes,
I give you my sprig of lilac.
(Nor for you, for one alone,
Blossoms and branches green to coffins all I bring,
For fresh as the morning, thus would I chant a song
      for you, O sane and sacred death.

All over bouquets of roses,
O death, I cover you over with roses and early lilies,
But mostly and now the lilac that blooms the first,
Copious I break, I break the sprigs from the bushes,
With loaded arms I come, pouring for you,
For you and the coffins, all of you, O death!)

VIII

O western orb sailing the heaven,
Now I know what you must have meant as a month
     since I walked,
As I walked in silence the transparent shadowy night,
As I saw you had something to tell as you bent to me
     night after night,
As you dropped from the sky low down as if to my
     side, (while the other stars all looked on,)
As we wandered together the solemn night, (for some-
     thing I know not what kept me from sleep,)
As the night advanced, and I saw on the rim of the
     west how full you were of woe,
As I stood on the rising ground in the breeze in the
     cool transparent night,
As I watched where you passed and was lost in the
     netherward black of the night,
As my soul in its trouble dissatisfied sank, as where
     you sad orb,
Concluded, dropt in the night, and was gone.

IX

Sing on there in the swamp,
O singer bashful and tender, I hear your notes, I hear
     your call,
I hear, I come presently, I understand you,
But a moment I linger, for the lustrous star has de-
     tained me,
The star my departing comrade holds and detains me.

X

O how shall I warble myself for the dead one there I
     loved?
And how shall I deck my song for the large sweet
     soul that has gone?
And what shall my perfume be for the grave of him
     I love?

Sea-winds blown from east and west,
Blown from the Eastern sea and blown from the West-
    ern sea, till there on the prairies meeting,
These and with these and the breath of my chant,
I'll perfume the grave of him I love.

XI

O what shall I hang on the chamber walls?
And what shall the pictures be that I hang on the
    walls,
To adorn the burial-house of him I love?
Pictures of growing spring and farms and homes,
With the Fourth-month eve at sundown, and the gray
    smoke lucid and bright,
With floods of the yellow gold of the gorgeous, indo-
    lent, sinking sun, burning, expanding the air,
With the fresh sweet herbage under foot, and the pale
    green leaves of the trees prolific,
In the distance the flowing glaze, the breast of the
    river, with a wind-dapple here and there,
With ranging hills on the banks, with many a line
    against the sky, and shadows,
And the city at hand with dwellings so dense, and
    stacks of chimneys,
And all the scenes of life and the workshops, and the
    workmen homeward returning.

XII

Lo, body and soul—this land,
My own Manhattan with spires, and the sparkling and
    hurrying tides, and the ships,
The varied and ample land, the South and the North
    in the light, Ohio's shores and flashing Mis-
    souri,
And ever the far-spreading prairies covered with grass
    and corn.

THE PRAISE OF LINCOLN

Lo, the most excellent sun so calm and haughty,
The violet and purple morn with just-felt breezes,
The gentle soft-born measureless light,
The miracle spreading bathing all, the fulfilled noon,
The coming eve delicious, the welcome night and the
    stars,
Over my cities shining all, enveloping man and land.

XIII

Sing on, sing on, you gray-brown bird,
Sing from the swamps, the recesses, pour your chant
    from the bushes,
Limitless out of the dusk, out of the cedars and pines.

Sing on, dearest brother, warble your reedy song,
Loud human song, with voice of uttermost woe.
O liquid and free and tender!
O wild and loose to my soul—O wondrous singer!
You only I hear—yet the star holds me, (but will soon
    depart,)
Yet the lilac with mastering odor holds me.

XIV

Now while I sat in the day and looked forth,
In the close of the day with its light and the fields of
    spring, and the farmers preparing their crops,
In the large unconscious scenery of my land with its
    lakes and forests,
In the heavenly aërial beauty, (after the perturbed
    winds and the storms,)
Under the arching heavens of the afternoon swift
    passing, and the voices of women and children,
The many moving sea-tides, and I saw the ships how
    they sailed,

And the summer approaching with richness, and the
 fields all busy with labor,
And the infinite separate houses, how they all went on,
 each with its meals and minutia of daily usages,
And the streets how their throbbings throbbed, and the
 cities pent—lo, then and there,
Falling upon them all, and among them all, enveloping
 me with the rest,
Appeared the cloud, appeared the long, black trail,
And I knew death, its thought, and the sacred knowledge of death.

Then with the knowledge of death as walking one side
 of me,
And the thought of death close-walking the other side
 of me,
And I in the middle as with companions, and as holding the hands of companions,
I fled forth to the hiding receiving night that talks not,
Down to the shores of the water, the path by the
 swamp in the dimness,
To the solemn shadowy cedars and the ghostly pines
 so still.

And the singer so shy to the rest received me,
The gray-brown bird I know received us comrades
 three,
And he sang the carol of death, and a verse for him I
 loved.

From deep secluded recesses,
From the fragrant cedars and the ghostly pines so still,
Came the carol of the bird.

And the charm of the carol rapt me,
As I held as if by their hands my comrades in the
 night,
And the voice of my spirit tallied the song of the bird.

Come lovely and soothing death,
Undulate round the world, serenely arriving, arriving,
In the day, in the night, to all, to each,
Sooner or later delicate death.

Praised be the fathomless universe,
For life and joy, and for objects and knowledge curi-
ous,
And for love, sweet love—but praise! praise! praise!
For the sure-enwinding arms of cool-enfolding death.

Dark mother always gliding near with soft feet,
Have none chanted for thee a chant of fullest wel-
come?
Then I chant it for thee, I glorify thee above all,
I bring thee a song that when thou must indeed come,
come unfalteringly.

Approach strong deliveress,
When it is so, when thou hast taken them I joyously
sing the dead,
Lost in the loving floating ocean of thee,
Laved in the flood of thy bliss, O death.

From me to thee glad serenades,
Dances for thee I propose saluting thee, adornments
and feastings for thee,
And the sights of the open landscape and the high-
spread sky are fitting,
And life and the fields, and the huge and thoughtful
night.

The night in silence under many a star,
The ocean shore and the husky whispering wave whose
voice I know,
And the soul turning to thee, O vast and well-veiled
death,
And the body gratefully nestling close to thee.

THE PRAISE OF LINCOLN

Over the tree-tops I float thee a song,
Over the rising and sinking waves, over the myriad
fields and the prairies wide,
Over the dense-packed cities all and the teeming
wharves and ways,
I float this carol with joy, with joy to thee, O death.

XV

To the tally of my soul,
Loud and strong kept up the gray-brown bird,
With pure deliberate notes spreading filling the night.
Loud in the pines and cedars dim,
Clear in the freshness moist and the swamp-perfume,
And I with my comrades there in the night.

While my sight that was bound in my eyes unclosed,
As to long panoramas of visions.

And I saw askant the armies,
I saw as in noiseless dreams hundreds of battle-flags,
Borne through the smoke of the battles and pierced
with missiles I saw them,
And carried hither and yon through the smoke, and
torn and bloody,
And at last but a few shreds left on the staffs, (and all
in silence,)
And the staffs all splintered and broken.

I saw battle-corpses, myriads of them,
And the white skeletons of young men, I saw them,
I saw the debris and debris of all the slain soldiers of
the war,
But I saw they were not as was thought,
They themselves were fully at rest, they suffered not,
The living remained and suffered, the mother suffered,
And the wife and the child and the musing comrade
suffered,
And the armies that remained suffered.

XVI

Passing the visions, passing the night,
Passing, unloosing the hold of my comrades' hands,
Passing the song of the hermit bird and the tallying
    song of my soul,
Victorious song, death's outlet song, yet varying ever-
    altering song,
As low and wailing, yet clear the notes, rising and
    falling, flooding the night,
Sadly sinking and fainting, as warning and warning,
    and yet again bursting with joy,
Covering the earth and filling the spread of the heav-
    ens,
As that powerful psalm in the night I heard from re-
    cesses,
Passing, I leave thee lilac with heart-shaped leaves,
I leave thee there in the dooryard, blooming, returning
    with spring.

I cease from my song for thee,
From my gaze on thee in the west, fronting the west,
    communing with thee,
O comrade lustrous with silver face in the night.

Yet each to keep and all, retrievements out of the
    night,
The song, the wondrous chant of the gray-brown bird,
And the tallying chant, the echo aroused in my soul,
With the lustrous and drooping star with the counte-
    nance full of woe,
With the holders holding my hand nearing the call of
    the bird,
Comrades mine and I in the midst, and their memory
    ever to keep, for the dead I loved so well,

THE PRAISE OF LINCOLN

For the sweetest, wisest soul of all my days and lands
    —and this for his dear sake,
Lilac and star and bird twined with the chant of my
    soul,
There in the fragrant pines and the cedars dusk and
    dim.

ANNIVERSARY OF THE BIRTH OF ABRAHAM LINCOLN

Levi Lewis Hager

(February 12th, 1900)

THIS day, upon the scroll of fame,
We venerate anew his name
Who healed the wound by brothers made,
When hostile armies did invade.

He fell a martyr for his land,
Struck down by the assassin's hand;
But rose immortal, like the star
Which sends its radiance from afar.

His praises for the jubilee
Which did a race from bondage free,
Will from that people ever rise,
Like holy incense, to the skies.

The nation great, united now,
With heads and hearts do grateful bow
To do him homage—let it be
The tribute of his country, free.

120

ACCOMPLICES

Thomas Bailey Aldrich

(Virginia, 1865)

THE soft new grass is creeping o'er the graves
   By the Potomac; and the crisp ground-flower
   Lifts its blue cup to catch the passing shower;
The pine-cone ripens, and the long moss waves
Its tangled gonfalons above our braves.
   Hark, what a burst of music from yon wood!
   The Southern nightingale, above its brood,
In its melodious summer madness raves.
Ah, with what delicate touches of her hand,
   With what sweet voices, Nature seeks to screen
The awful Crime of this distracted land,—
   Sets her birds singing, while she spreads her green
Mantle of velvet where the Murdered lie,
As if to hide the horror from God's eye!

THE BIRTHDAY OF ABRAHAM LINCOLN

Mary A. Leavitt

FROM the tints and the tones of other years,
   From the bloom of the Far Away,
What chaplets grateful Memory weaves
   On this anniversary day!

How we hear the tramp of marching feet
   And the call of the bugle blast;
And the glad acclaim as the troops come home,
   When the terrible war is past!

THE PRAISE OF LINCOLN

In the midst of joy, we hear the toll—
 The toll of a funeral bell!
From around the globe comes a wail of woe
 That blends in one funeral knell!

Joy is struck dead by a crushing blow!
 The nation's deliverer slain!
No wonder each heart is whelmed in grief
 And each wind bears a sob of pain!

Hallow his tomb, O Illinois!
 Still sacred keep that shrine
Where love would twine immortal wreaths,
 And blend her gifts with thine.

O peerless Leader! but prized too late!
 Strange tear-dimmed eyes now see it all!
Abused by foes, misknown by friends—
 Too late, too late, our praises fall!

LINCOLN'S BIRTHDAY

Ida Vose Woodbury

AGAIN thy birthday dawns, O man beloved,
 Dawns on the land thy blood was shed to save,
And hearts of millions, by one impulse moved,
 Bow and fresh laurels lay upon thy grave.

The years but add new luster to thy glory,
 And watchmen on the heights of vision see
Reflected in thy life the old, old story,
 The story of the Man of Galilee.

THE PRAISE OF LINCOLN

We see in thee the image of Him kneeling
    Before the close-shut tomb, and at the word
"Come forth," from out the blackness long concealing
    There rose a man; clearly again was heard

The Master's voice, and then, his cerements broken,
    Friends of the dead a living brother see;
Thou, at the tomb where millions lay, hast spoken:
    "Loose him and let him go!"—the slave was free.

And in the man so long in thraldom hidden
    We see the likeness of the Father's face,
Clod changed to soul; by thy atonement bidden,
    We hasten to the uplift of a race.

Spirit of Lincoln! Summon all thy loyal;
    Nerve them to follow where thy feet have trod,
To prove, by voice as clear and deed as royal,
    Man's brotherhood in our one Father—God.

LINCOLN'S BIRTHDAY

Nathan Haskell Dole

(February 12th, 1809)

As BACK we look across the ages
    A few great figures meet the eye—
Kings, prophets, warriors, poets, sages—
    Whose names and deeds will never die.

The rest are all forgotten, perished,
    Like trees in trackless forests vast,
But those whose memory men have cherished
    Seem living still and have no past.

THE PRAISE OF LINCOLN

Not always of high race or royal
  These messengers of God to men,
But lowly-born, true-hearted, loyal,
  They wielded sword or brush or pen.

Such was our Lincoln, who forever
  Is hailed as Freer of the Slave,
Whose lofty purpose and endeavor
  New hope to hopeless bondmen gave.

Gaunt, hewed as if from rugged boulders,
  He bore a world of care and woe,
Which creased his brow and bent his shoulders,
  And as a martyr laid him low.

And so we tell our sons his story,
  We celebrate his humble birth,
And crown his deeds with all the glory
  That men can offer on this earth.

Hail, Lincoln! As the swift years lengthen
  Still more majestic grows thy fame;
The ties that bind us to thee strengthen;
  Starlike-immortal shines thy name.

ON READING
PRESIDENT LINCOLN'S LETTER

H. L. Gordon

(Written to Horace Greeley, of Date August 22d, 1862: "If I
could save the union without freeing any slave,
I would do it," etc.)

PERISH the power that, bowed to dust,
  Still wields a tyrant's rod—
That dares not even then be just,
  And leave the rest with God.

ABRAHAM LINCOLN

Henry Howard Brownell

DEAD is the roll of the drums,
  And the distant thunders die,
  They fade in the far-off sky;
And a lovely summer comes,
  Like the smile of Him on high.

Lulled, the storm and the onset,
  Earth lies in a sunny swoon;
  Stiller splendor of noon,
Softer glory of sunset,
  Milder starlight and moon!

For the kindly Seasons love us;
  They smile over trench and clod
(Where we left the bravest of us,)—
  There's a brighter green of the sod,
And a holier calm above us
  In the blessed Blue of God.

The roar and the ravage were vain;
  And Nature, that never yields,
Is busy with sun and rain
  At her old sweet work again
  On the lonely battle-fields.

How the tall white daisies grow,
  Where the grim artillery rolled!
(Was it only a moon ago?
  It seems a century old,)—

And the bee hums in the clover,
　As the pleasant June comes on;
Aye, the wars are all over,—
　But our good Father is gone.

There was tumbling of traitor fort,
　Flaming of traitor fleet—
Lighting of city and port,
　Clasping in square and street.

There was thunder of mine and gun,
　Cheering by mast and tent,—
When—his dread work all done,
And his high fame full won—
　Died the Good President.

In his quiet chair he sate,
　Pure of malice or guile,
Stainless of fear or hate,—
　And there played a pleasant smile
On the rough and careworn face;
　For his heart was all the while
On means of mercy and grace.

The brave old Flag drooped o'er him,
　(A fold in the hard hand lay,)—
　He looked, perchance, on the play,—
But the scene was a shadow before him,
　For his thoughts were far away.

'Twas but the morn, (yon fearful
　Death-shade, gloomy and vast,
　Lifting slowly at last,)
　His household heard him say,
" 'Tis long since I've been so cheerful,
　So light of heart as to-day."

THE PRAISE OF LINCOLN

'Twas dying, the long dread clang,—
But, or ever the blessed ray
Of peace could brighten to-day,
Murder stood by the way—
Treason struck home his fang!
One throb—and, without a pang,
That pure soul passed away.

Kindly Spirit!—Ah, when did treason
Bid such a generous nature cease,
Mild by temper and strong by reason,
But ever leaning to love and peace?
A head how sober; a heart how spacious;
A manner equal with high or low;
Rough but gentle, uncouth but gracious,
And still inclining to lips of woe.

Patient when saddest, calm when sternest,
Grieved when rigid for justice' sake;
Given to jest, yet ever in earnest
If aught of right or truth were at stake.

Simple of heart, yet shrewd therewith,
Slow to resolve, but firm to hold;
Still with parable and with myth
Seasoning truth, like Them of old;
Aptest humor and quaintest pith!
(Still we smile o'er the tales he told.)

Yet whoso might pierce the guise
Of mirth in the man we mourn,
Would mark, and with grieved surprise,
All the great soul had borne,
In the piteous lines, and the kind, sad eyes
So dreadfully wearied and worn.

127

And we trusted (the last dread page
   Once turned, of our Dooms-day Scroll,)
   To have seen him, sunny of soul,
In a cheery, grand old age.

But, Father, 'tis well with thee!
   And since ever, when God draws nigh,
Some grief for the mood must be,
   'Twas well, even so to die,—

'Mid the thunder of Treason's fall,
   The yielding of haughty town,
The crashing of cruel wall,
   The trembling of tyrant crown!

The ringing of hearth and pavement
   To the clash of falling chains,—
The centuries of enslavement
   Dead, with their blood-bought gains!

And through trouble weary and long,
   Well hadst thou seen the way,
Leaving the State so strong
   It did not reel for a day;

And even in death couldst give
   A token for Freedom's strife—
A proof how republics live,
   And not by a single life,

But the Right Divine of man,
   And the many, trained to be free,—
And none, since the world began,
   Ever was mourned like thee.

THE PRAISE OF LINCOLN

Dost thou feel it, O noble Heart!
    (So grieved and so wronged below,)
From the rest wherein thou art?
Do they see it, those patient eyes?
Is there heed in the happy skies
    For tokens of world-wide woe?

The Land's great lamentations,
    The mighty mourning of cannon,
        The myriad flags half-mast—
The last remorse of the nations,
    Grief from Volga to Shannon!
        (Now they know thee at last.)

How, from gray Niagara's shore
    To Canaveral's surfy shoal—
From the rough Atlantic roar
    To the long Pacific roll—
    For bereavement and for dole,
Every cottage wears its weed,
    White as thine own pure soul,—
And black as the traitor deed.

How, under a nation's pall,
    The dust so dear in our sight
        To its home on the prairie past,—
The leagues of funeral,
    The myriads, morn and night,
        Pressing to look their last.

Nor alone the State's Eclipse;
    But tears in hard eyes gather—
And on rough and bearded lips,
Of the regiments and the ships—
    "Oh, our dear Father!"

And methinks of all the million
    That looked on the dark dead face,
'Neath its sable-plumed pavilion,
    The crone of a humbler race
Is saddest of all to think on,
    And the old swart lips that said,
Sobbing, "Abraham Lincoln!
    Oh, he is dead, he is dead!"

Hush! let our heavy souls
    To-day be glad; for again
The stormy music swells and rolls,
    Stirring the hearts of men.

And under the Nation's Dome,
    They've guarded so well and long,
Our boys come marching home,
    Two hundred thousand strong.

All in the pleasant month of May,
    With war-worn colors and drums,
Still through the livelong summer's day,
    Regiment, regiment comes.

Like the tide, yeasty and barmy,
    That sets on a wild lee-shore,
Surge the ranks of an army
    Never reviewed before!

Who shall look on the like again,
    Or see such host of the brave?
A mighty River of marching men
    Rolls the Capital through—
Rank on rank, and wave on wave,
    Of bayonet-crested blue!

THE PRAISE OF LINCOLN

How the chargers neigh and champ,
(Their riders weary of camp),
   With curvet and with caracole!—
The cavalry comes with thund'rous tramp,
   And the cannons heavily roll.

And ever, flowery and gay,
The Staff sweeps on in a spray
   Of tossing forelocks and manes;
But each bridle-arm has a weed
Of funeral, black as the steed
   That fiery Sheridan reins.

Grandest of mortal sights
   The sun-browned ranks to view—
The Colors ragg'd in a hundred fights,
   And the dusty Frocks of Blue!

And all day, mile on mile,
With cheer, and waving, and smile,
The war-worn legions defile
   Where the nation's noblest stand;
And the Great Lieutenant looks on,
   With the Flower of a rescued land,—
For the terrible work is done,
And the Good Fight is won
   For God and the Fatherland.

So, from the fields they win,
   Our men are marching home,
   A million are marching home!
To the cannon's thundering din,
   And banners on mast and dome,—
And the ships come sailing in
With all their ensigns dight,
As erst for a great sea-fight.

THE PRAISE OF LINCOLN

Let every color fly,
  Every pennon flaunt in pride;
Wave, Starry Flag, on high!
Float in the sunny sky,
  Stream o'er the stormy tide!
For every stripe of stainless hue,
And every star in the field of blue,
Ten thousand of the brave and true
  Have laid them down and died.

And in all our pride to-day
  We think, with a tender pain,
Of those so far away
  They will not come home again.

And our boys had fondly thought,
  To-day, in marching by,
From the ground so dearly bought,
And the fields so bravely fought,
  To have met their Father's eye.

But they may not see him in place,
  Nor their ranks be seen of him;
We look for the well-known face,
  And the splendor is strangely dim.

Perished?—who was it said
  Our Leader had passed away?
Dead? Our President dead?
  He has not died for a day!

We mourn for a little breath
  Such as, late or soon, dust yields;
But the Dark Flower of Death
  Blooms in the fadeless fields.

THE PRAISE OF LINCOLN

We looked on a cold, still brow,
  But Lincoln could yet survive;
  He never was more alive,
Never nearer than now.

For the pleasant season found him,
  Guarded by faithful hands,
  In the fairest of Summer Lands;
With his own brave staff around him,
  There our President stands.

There they are all at his side,
  The noble hearts and true,
  That did all men might do—
Then slept, with their swords, and died.

And around—(for there can cease
  This earthly trouble)—they throng,
The friends that have passed in peace,
  The foes that have seen their wrong.

(But, a little from the rest,
  With sad eyes looking down,
  And brows of softened frown,
With stern arms on the chest,
Are two, standing abreast—
  Stonewall and Old John Brown.)

But the stainless and the true,
  These by their President stand,
To look on his last review,
  Or march with the old command.

And lo! from a thousand fields,
  From all the old battle-haunts,
A greater Army than Sherman wields,
  A grander Review than Grant's.

THE PRAISE OF LINCOLN

Gathered home from the grave,
　Risen from sun and rain—
Rescued from wind and wave
　Out of the stormy main—
The Legions of our Brave
　Are all in their lines again!

Many a stout Corps that went,
Full-ranked, from camp and tent,
　And brought back a brigade;
Many a brave regiment,
　That mustered only a squad.

The lost battalions,
　That, when the fight went wrong,
Stood and died at their guns,—
　The stormers steady and strong,

With their best blood that bought
　Scarp, and ravelin, and wall,—
The companies that fought
　Till a corporal's guard was all.

Many a valiant crew,
　That passed in battle and wreck,—
Ah, so faithful and true!
　They died on the bloody deck,
They sank in the soundless blue.

All the loyal and bold
　That lay on a soldier's bier,—
　The stretchers borne to the rear,
The hammocks lowered to the hold.

The shattered wreck we hurried,
　In death-fight, from deck and port,—
The Blacks that Wagner buried—
　That died in the Bloody Fort!

134

THE PRAISE OF LINCOLN

Comrades of camp and mess,
  Left, as they lay, to die,
In the battle's sorest stress,
  When the storm of fight swept by,—
They lay in the Wilderness,
  Ah, where did they not lie?

In the tangled swamp they lay,
  They lay so still on the sward!—
They rolled in the sick-bay,
Moaning their lives away—
  They flushed in the fevered ward.

They rotted in Libby yonder,
  They starved in the foul stockade—
Hearing afar the thunder
  Of the Union cannonade!

But the old wounds all are healed,
  And the dungeoned limbs are free,—
The Blue Frocks rise from the field,
  The Blue Jackets out of the sea.

They've 'scaped from the torture-den,
  They've broken the bloody sod,
They've all come to life again!—
The Third of a Million men
  That died for Thee and God!

A tenderer green than May
  The Eternal Season wears,—
The blue of our summer's day
  Is dim and pallid to theirs,—
The Horror faded away,
  And 'twas heaven all unawares!

135

Tents on the Infinite Shore!
   Flags in the azuline sky,
Sails on the seas once more!
   To-day, in the heaven on high,
All under arms once more!

The troops are all in their lines,
   The guidons flutter and play;
But every bayonet shines,
   For all must march to-day.

What lofty pennons flaunt?
What mighty echoes haunt,
   As of great guns, o'er the main?
   Hark to the sound again—
The *Congress* is all a-taunt!
   The *Cumberland's* manned again!

All the ships and their men
   Are in line of battle to-day,—
All at quarters, as when
   Their last roll thundered away,—
All at their guns, as then,
   For the Fleet salutes to-day.

The armies have broken camp
   On the vast and sunny plain,
   The drums are rolling again;
With steady, measured tramp,
   They're marching all again.

With alignment firm and solemn,
   Once again they form
In mighty square and column,—
   But never for charge and storm.

THE PRAISE OF LINCOLN

The Old Flag they died under
    Floats above them on the shore,
'And on the great ships yonder
    The ensigns dip once more—
And once again the thunder
    Of the thirty guns and four!

In solid platoons of steel,
    Under heaven's triumphal arch,
The long lines break and wheel—
    And the word is, "Forward, march!"

The Colors ripple o'erhead,
    The drums roll up to the sky,
And with martial time and tread
    The regiments all pass by—
The ranks of our faithful Dead,
    Meeting their President's eye.

With a soldier's quiet pride
    They smile o'er the perished pain,
    For their anguish was not vain—
For thee, O Father, we died!
    And we did not die in vain.

March on, your last brave mile!
    Salute him, Star and Lace,
Form round him, rank and file,
    And look on the kind, rough face;
But the quaint and homely smile
    Has a glory and a grace
It never had known erewhile—
    Never, in time and space.

THE PRAISE OF LINCOLN

On chime of eight precise, gaunt, bare of head,
They saw his tallness in the balcony-flare,
And straightway all the murmurous street grew still,
Till silence absolute as death befell.

And in that perfect silence one clear voice
Inspired began, from out the multiude,
The song of all the songs of all the war,
Simple, ecstatic, sacrificial, strong—
"We're coming, Father Abraham, three hundred thou-
        sand more"—
And neighboring voices took the long refrain
While some more distant raised the opening words,
Till to and fro and far and near at once,
Never in chorus, chanting as by groups,
Here ending, there beginning, some halfway,
All sang at once, and all renewing all
In pledge and passion of the mighty song,
Their different words and clashing cadences
Wondrously merging in a sound supreme,
As if the inmost meaning of the hymn
Harmonious rolled in one unending vow
While all the singers gazed on Lincoln's face.

Hands gripping balcony-rail, he stooped and saw
And listened motionless, with such a look
The boy upon the lamp-post clearly knew
"The heavens were opened unto him,"—
"The spirit of God descending like a dove"—
Until the mystery of the general soul
Wrought to unwonted sense of unison
Moved all to silence for the homely words
Of Father Abraham Lincoln to his kind—
Words clear as Light itself, so plain—so plain
None deemed him other than their fellow man.

THE PRAISE OF LINCOLN

III

Once more. A boy in blue at sixteen years,
Mid groups of blue along the crazy road
Of corduroy astretch from City Point,
Toward yonder spire in fatal Petersburg,
Beyond what trenches, rifle-pits, and forts,
What woeful far-front grave-mounds sunken down
To puddles over pickets shot on post—
What cemeteries shingle-marked with names
Of companies and regiments and corps,
Of moldering bones and rags of blue and gray,
And belts and buttons, rain and wind exposed—
Mired army wagons—forms of swollen mules—
Springfields and Enfields, broken-stocked, stuck up
Or strown, all rusting—parked artillery—
Brush shelter stables—lines and lines of huts,
Tent-covered winter quarters, sticks and mud
For chimneys to the many thousand smokes
Whose dropping cinders black-rimmed million holes
Through veteran canvas ludicrously patched—
Squares of parade all mud—and mud, and mud,
With mingled grass and chips and refuse cans
Strown myriad far about the plain of war,
Whose scrub-oak roots for scanty fires were grubbed,
And one sole house, and never fence remained
Where fifty leagues of corn-land smiled before.

Belated March—a lowering, rainless day
With glints of shine; the veteran tents of Meade
Gave forth their veteran boys in crowds of blue,
Infantry, cavalry, gunners, engineers,
Easterner, Westerner, Yankee, Irish, "Dutch,"
Canuck, all sorts and sizes, frowsed, unkempt,
Unwashed, half-smoked, profane exceedingly,
Moody or jokeful, formidable, free
From fear of colonels as of corporals,

141

THE PRAISE OF LINCOLN

Called Law, to save the one perennial Wrong—
That fundamental social crime which fates
All babes alike to Inequality,
And so condemns the many million minds
(That might, with happier nurture, finely serve)
To share, through life, the harmful hates or scorns
The accursed System breeds, which still most hurts
The few who fancy it their benefit,
Shutting them lifelong from the happiness
Of such close sympathy with all their kind
As feels the universal God, or Soul,
Alive to love in every human heart.

Was it for this our Mothers' sons were slain?
Shall Father Abraham not prevail again?

We who are marching to the small-flagged graves
We earned by fight to free our fathers' slaves,
We who by Lincoln's hero soul were sworn,
We go more sadly toward our earthly bourne
To join our comrade host of long ago,
Since, oh so clearly, do our old hearts know
We shall not witness what we longed to see—
Our own dear children minded to be free.

Why let democracy be flouted down?
Why let your money-mongers more renown
Their golden idol than the Common Weal,
Flaunting the gains of liberty-to-steal,
Fouling the promise of the heights we trod
With Freedom's sacrifice to Lincoln's God?

Was it for this he wept his children slain?
Or shall our Father's spirit rise again?

144

ABRAHAM LINCOLN

Florence Evelyn Pratt

LINCOLN, the woodsman, in the clearing stood,
　Hemmed by the solemn forest stretching round;
Stalwart, ungainly, honest-eyed and rude,
　The genius of that solitude profound.
He clove the way that future millions trod,
　He passed, unmoved by worldly fear or pelf;
In all his lusty toil he found not God,
　Though in the wilderness he found himself.

Lincoln, the President, in bitter strife,
　Best-loved, worst-hated of all living men,
Oft single-handed, for the nation's life
　Fought on, nor rested ere he fought again.
With one unerring purpose armed, he clove
　Through selfish sin; then overwhelmed with care,
His great heart sank beneath its load of love;
　Crushed to his knees, he found his God in prayer.

A LINCOLN CAMPAIGN SONG

(1858)

　WE hear a cry increasing still,
　Like light it springs from hill to hill—
　From Pennsylvania's State it leaps,
　And o'er the Buckeye valley sweeps.
　　Get out of the way, Stephen Douglas!
　　Get out of the way, Stephen Douglas!
　　Get out of the way, Stephen Douglas!
　　Lincoln is the man we want to serve us!

145

THE PRAISE OF LINCOLN

Hoosier State first caught the cry,
The Hawkeye State then raised it high,
The Sucker State now waits the day,
When Lincoln leads to victory!
    Get out of the way, Stephen Douglas!
    Get out of the way, Stephen Douglas!
    Get out of the way, Stephen Douglas!
    Lincoln is the man we want to serve us!

Cheer up, for victory's on its way,
No power its onward march can stay,
As well to stop the thunder's roar
As hope for Doug to serve us more.
    Get out of the way, Stephen Douglas!
    Get out of the way, Stephen Douglas!
    Get out of the way, Stephen Douglas!
    Lincoln is the man we want to serve us!

Then, Freemen, rally, one and all,
Respond to our brave leader's call;
Free Speech, Free Press, Free Soil, want we,
And Lincoln to lead for liberty!
    Get out of the way, Stephen Douglas!
    Get out of the way, Stephen Douglas!
    Get out of the way, Stephen Douglas!
    Lincoln is the man we want to serve us!

LINCOLN

John Townsend Trowbridge

HEROIC soul, in homely garb half hid,
  Sincere, sagacious, melancholy, quaint;
What he endured, no less than what he did,
  Has reared his monument, and crowned him saint.

DOUGLAS' COMPLAINT

(1860)

HE punished me—in fight you see,
    And said I had the wrong of it;
For I am small and he is tall,
    And that's the short and long of it.

He split a rail, through my coat-tail
    He quickly thrust the prong of it;
I'm five feet one, that lofty son
    Is six feet four and strong of it.

"WIDE-AWAKE CLUB" SONG

(Tune: "A Wet Sail and a Flowing Sea")

OH, hear you not the wild huzzas
    That come from every State?
For honest Uncle Abraham,
    The people's candidate?

He is our choice, our nominee,
    A self-made man and true;
We'll show the Democrats this fall
    What honest Abe can do.

Then give us Abe, and Hamlin, too,
    To guide our gallant ship,
With Seward, Sumner, Chase, and Clay,
    And then a merry trip.

I hear that Doug is half inclined
    To give us all leg-bail,
Preferring exercise on foot
    To riding on a rail.

For Abe has one already mauled
   Upon the White House plan;
If once Doug gets astride of that,
   He is a used up man.

Then give us Abe, and Hamlin, too,
   To guide our gallant ship,
With Seward, Sumner, Chase, and Clay,
   And then a merry trip.

HONEST ABE

Henry Howard Brownell

(Nomination of 1860. "A Most Hideous Nickname")

"Honest Abe!" What strange vexation
   Thrills an office-armchaired party!
What impatience and disgust
That the people should put trust
   In a name so true and hearty!
What indignant lamentation
   For the unchose—surely fitter
   (*Growl they*) than a rough rail-splitter—
Most unheard-of nomination!

If the name you chance to mention,
Sir (*they splutter*) the Convention,
   Sir, has acted like a babe!
You have missed it, be assured,
All your best men left to leeward;
Give us Banks, or Bates, or Seward—
   But confound this "Honest Abe!"

THE PRAISE OF LINCOLN

There's a story somewhere told,
By a fellow grave and old,
    Which, just now, is rather pat.
I bethink me of his name—
Plutarch—and of lives the same
    Had as many as a cat.

In the little state of Athens
    Was a usage, there and then
Practiced by those classic heathens,
    Rather hard on public men.
Whatsoe'er the service past,
    If they happened to distrust 'em—
Thought 'em getting on too fast—
    'Twas, it seems, the pleasant custom
Just an oyster-shell to shy
(*Sans* a wherefore or a why)
Into a ballot-box huge and high—
    With whatever name upon it,
Chanced the elector's mind to strike,
    (Sulking, like a jealous noddy,
    O'er his Norways and his toddy,)—
    Well, the name of anybody
That he didn't chance to like.
    And the gentleman who won it—
Such election—(held to tell
    What the free enlightened wished)
    Was, in fact, considered dished,
And served out on the half-shell!
    And must needs, at any rate,
Draw a line in double-quick,
Mizzle, vamos, cut his stick,
    And absquatulate!

149

THE PRAISE OF LINCOLN

Simple and ingenious scheme!
  Of split tickets there were none—
'(Though the bivalve you might deem
Suited well for such extreme)—
  Hard or Soft Shell—all were one!

Once, while thus with general clamor
  Athens eased her factious heart—
When the smith forsook his hammer,
  And the huckster left his mart—
Past the scene of noisy riot,
  Clatter of shells and windy talk,
Aristides, calm and quiet,
  Chanced to take a morning walk.

Musing, in his wonted fashion,
  On the double care of state—
On the Demos' fickle passion,
  And the cold patrician hate—

When a voter pressed beside him,
  Saying, "Stranger, can you spell
Aristides? Wal, jest write him,
  Square and straight, on this here shell."

Smiling, cheery as a cricket,
  Wrote the old Republican—
Then, as he returned the ticket,
  Asked—"And what's his crime, my man?"

"Wal, not much," said Snooks, appearing
  Puzzled, "only I'll be cussed
But I'm sick to death of hearing
  That old critter called *'The Just!'* "

PARRICIDE

Julia Ward Howe

(Abraham Lincoln—April 14th, 1865)

O'ER the warrior gauntlet grim
Late the silken glove we drew,
Bade the watch-fires slacken dim
In the dawn's auspicious hue.
    Stayed the armed heel;
    Still the clanging steel;
Joys unwonted thrilled the silence through.

Gladly drew the Easter tide;
And the thoughts of men anew
Turned to Him who spotless died
For the peace that none shall rue.
    Out of mortal pain
    This abiding strain
Issued: "Peace, my peace I give to you."

Musing o'er the silent strings,
By their apathy oppressed,
Waiting for the spirit-wings
To be touched and soul-possessed.
    "I am dull," I said:
    "Treason is not dead;
Still in ambush lurks the shivering guest."

Then a woman's shriek of fear
Smote us in its arrowy flight;
And a wonder wild and drear
Did the hearts of men unite.
    Has the seed of crime
    Reached its flowering-time,
That it shoots to this audacious height?

Then, as frosts the landscape change,
Stiffening from the summer's glow,
Grew the jocund faces strange,
Lay the loftiest emblem low:
      Kings are of the past,
      Suffered still to last;
These twin crowns the present did bestow.

Fair assassin, murder white,
With thy serpent speed avoid
Each unsullied household light,
Every conscience unalloyed.
      Neither heart nor home
      Where good angels come
Suffer thee in nearness to abide.

Slanderer of the gracious brow,
The untiring blood of youth,
Servant of an evil vow,
Of a crime that beggars ruth,
      Treason was thy dam,
      Wolfling, when the Lamb,
The Anointed, met thy venomed tooth.

With the righteous did he fall,
With the sainted doth he lie;
While the gibbet's vultures call
Thee, that, 'twixt the earth and sky,
      Disavowed of both
      In their Godward troth,
Thou mayst make thy poor amend, and die.

THE PRAISE OF LINCOLN

If it were my latest breath,
Doomed his bloody end to share,
I would brand thee with his death
As a deed beyond despair.
 Since the Christ was lost
 For a felon's cost,
None like thee of vengeance should beware.

Leave the murderer, noble song,
Helpless in the toils of fate:
To the just thy meeds belong,
To the martyr, to the state,
 When the storms beat loud
 Over sail and shroud,
Tunefully the seaman cheers his mate.

Never tempest lashed the wave
But to leave it fresher calm;
Never weapon scarred the brave
But their blood did purchase balm.
 God hath writ on high
 Such a victory
As uplifts the nation with its psalm.

Honor to the heart of love,
Honor to the peaceful will,
Slow to threaten, strong to move,
Swift to render good for ill!
 Glory crowns his end,
 And the captive's friend
From his ashes makes us freemen still.

PARDON

Julia Ward Howe

(Wilkes Booth—April 26th, 1865)

PAINS the sharp sentence the heart in whose wrath it
    was uttered,
           Now thou art cold;
Vengeance, the headlong, and Justice, with purpose
    close muttered,
           Loosen their hold.

Death brings atonement; he did that whereof ye ac-
    cuse him,—
           Murder accurst;
But from that crisis of crime in which Satan did lose
    him,
           Suffered the worst.

Harshly the red dawn arose on a deed of his doing,
           Never to mend;
But harsher days he wore out in the bitter pursuing
           And the wild end.

So lift the pale flag of truce, wrap those mysteries
    round him,
           In whose avail
Madness that moved, and the swift retribution that
    found him,
           Falter and fail.

So the soft purples that quiet the heavens with mourn-
    ing
           Willing to fall,
Lend him one fold, his illustrious victim adorning
           With wider pall.

THE PRAISE OF LINCOLN

Back to the cross, where the Savior uplifted in dying
    Bade all souls live,
Turns the reft bosom of Nature, his mother, low sigh-
    ing,
        Greatest, forgive!

LINCOLN

Richard Linthicum

(On the Fiftieth Anniversary of His Nomination for President
of the United States, May 18th, 1860—1910)

The Beginning

WHAT strong, sure hand shall guide the laboring ship
Through seas that gather rage beneath black skies
And bring a new world's freighted hopes to port?
Give us a captain bold and tried and true,
Not this gaunt, shambling, homespun lout—
Railsplitter, backwoods jester, wrestling clown.

The End

A sturdy oak knit to the virgin soil,
Its sheltering boughs in benediction spread
And nerve-responsive to each gentle breeze,
Storm-racked and bent, the forest's pride and chief,
Outlives the tempest and the lightning's wrath
To die in its full prime, stung by a worm.

The Retrospect

As in a mountain range one giant peak
Lifts its tall head above its fellow-crests,
A guide to all within the lofty land,
A world-enriching treasure in its depths,
So Lincoln stood among his fellow-men,
With rugged, seamy front and heart of gold.

LINCOLN

Lydia Landon Elliott

THE deeds of him who bore that name
On Ethiopia's soul are marked in flame!
Caressed at birth by Toil's hard hands,
He lingered not, till Life's uplands
Rose clear, distinct before his gaze—
A golden mist from purplish haze.
Honesty, faith, pure love, exemplified;
Great Nature wept when Lincoln died!

ABRAHAM LINCOLN

Walter Malone

A BLEND of mirth and sadness, smiles and tears;
A quaint knight-errant of the pioneers;
A homely hero born of star and sod;
A Peasant Prince; a Masterpiece of God.

LINCOLN—THE BOY

James Whitcomb Riley

O SIMPLE as the rhymes that tell
    The simplest tales of youth,
Or simple as a miracle
    Beside the simplest truth—
So simple seems the view we share
    With our Immortals, sheer
From Glory looking down to where
    They were as children here.

156

THE PRAISE OF LINCOLN

Or thus we know, nor doubt it not,
    The boy he must have been
Whose budding heart bloomed with the thought
    All men are kith and kin—
With love-light in his eyes and shade
    Of prescient tears:—Because
Only of such a boy were made
    The loving man he was.

THE STROKE OF JUSTICE

Lyman Whitney Allen

THE hour was come, the Nation's crucial hour;
    A crisis of the world, a turn of time;
      The ages' hope and dream.
And one undaunted soul, sinewed with power,
    Freedom's anointed, rose to height sublime,
      Imperial and supreme;

And, lifting high o'er groaning multitude
    His sovereign scepter, smote with such a stroke
      The chains of centuries,
That earth was shaken to its farthest rood;
    That million manacles asunder broke,
      And myriad properties

Became, in one immortal moment,—men;
    Free with the free in all the rounded earth;
      Redeemed by martyr blood;
To stand with faces to the light again,
    Attaining, through their resurrection birth,
      To human brotherhood.

157

LINCOLN

Thomas MacKellar

So DEEP our grief, it may be silence is
    The meetest tribute to the father's name:
A secret shrine in every heart is his
    Whom death hath girt with an immortal fame;
And in this dim recess our thoughts abide,
    Clad in the garment of unspoken grief,
As fain the sorrow of the heart to hide
    That yields no tears to give our woe relief.
But death is not to such as he, we cry:
    His tongue is mute; his heart may pulse no more:
Yet men so good and loved do never die;
    But while the tide shall flow upon the shore
Of time to come, a presence to the eye
    Of nations shall he be, and evermore
Shall freemen treasure in historic page
This martyr-hero of earth's noblest age.

ABRAHAM LINCOLN

Rose Terry Cooke

("Strangulatus Pro Republica")

HUNDREDS there have been, loftier than their kind,
    Heroes and victors in the world's great wars:
    Hundreds, exalted as the eternal stars,
By the great heart, or keen and mighty mind;
There have been sufferers, maimed and halt and blind,
    Who bore their woes in such triumphant calm
    That God hath crowned them with the martyr's
        palm;
And there were those who fought through fire to find

Their Master's face, and were by fire refined.
  But who like thee, oh Sire! hath ever stood
Steadfast for truth and right, when lies and wrong
Rolled their dark waters, turbulent and strong;
  Who bore reviling, baseness, tears and blood
Poured out like water, till thine own was spent,
Then reaped Earth's sole reward—a grave and monu-
    ment!

LINCOLN: A RETROSPECT

Harry H. Kemp

Now that the winds of Peace have blown away
The battle smoke which long obscured the day,
Now that all wrath is as a tale of old
And human flesh is minted into gold
No longer, and the straggling thunders cease
And all the land is wrapt in busy peace—
There towers in our sight this man of worth
Above the selfish kings that ruled the earth.
He did not yearn for hopeless things, nor sigh
For purple kingdoms verging on the sky,
Nor long for irised landscapes shimmering fair
In a blown bubble of inconstant air,
But with great vision of the years to be
He shaped a mighty nation's destiny
And gave all man can give—his life he gave—
To weld the broken state and free the slave.

Gave resolution to the ruler's pen;
The books he conned beside the open fire
Made strong the brain which battles could not tire;
The law courts with forensic shift and strife
The ax the gaunt youth swung in dale and glen
Prepared him for that tragedy, his life.

THE PRAISE OF LINCOLN

He never held his ways from men apart,
Yet kept a sanctuary in his heart
Whence flowed a stream of love and hope, to bless,
Pure as a clear spring in a wilderness.
He trusted God—bearing the weight of war—
As olden captains trusted in a star.
And yet he was not all the stolid oak:
Full well could he the foeman's smile provoke
With homely proverb or a timely joke.

Calm and serene unto the end he passed
And bravely met his martyrdom at last. . . .
They crossed his thin, worn hands upon his breast.
God gave the country peace and Lincoln rest!

ABRAHAM LINCOLN

John Vance Cheney

His people called, and forth he came
As one that answers to his name;
Nor dreamed how high his charge,
His privilege how large,—

To set the stones back in the wall
Lest the divided house should fall.
The shepherd who would keep
The flocks, would fold the sheep,

Humbly he came, yet with the mien
Presaging the immortal scene,—
Some battle of His wars
Who sealeth up the stars.

THE PRAISE OF LINCOLN

No flaunting of the banners bold
Borne by the haughty sons of old;
Their blare, their pageantries,
Their goal,—they were not his.

We called, he came; he came to crook
The spear into the pruning-hook,
To toil, untimely sleep,
And leave a world to weep.

LINCOLN

James G. Clark

WITH life unsullied from his youth,
    He meekly took the ruler's rod,
And, wielding it in love and truth,
    He lived, the noblest work of God.
He knew no fierce, unbalanced zeal,
    That spurns all human differings,
Nor craven fear that shuns the steel
    That carves the way to better things.

And in the night of blood and grief,
    When horror rested on the ark,
His was the calm, undimmed belief
    That felt God's presence in the dark;
Full well he knew each wandering star,
    That once had decked the azure dome
Would tremble through the clouds of War,
    And, like a prodigal, come home.

He perished ere the angel Peace
    Had rolled war's curtains from the sky,
But he shall live when wars shall cease—
    The great and good can never die;

THE PRAISE OF LINCOLN

For though his heart lies cold and still
  We feel its beatings warm and grand,
'And still his spirit pulses thrill
  Through all the councils of the land.

Oh, for the hosts that sleep to-day,
  Lulled by the sound of Southern waves;
The sun that lit them in the fray
  Now warms the flowers upon their graves—
Sweet flowers that speak like words of love
  Between the forms of friend and foe,
Perchance their spirits meet above,
  Who crossed their battle-blades below.

'Twas not in vain the deluge came,
  And systems crumbled in the gloom,
And not in vain have sword and flame
  Robbed home and heart of life and bloom;
The mourner's cross, the martyr's blood,
  Shall crown the world with holier rights,
And slavery's storm and slavery's flood
  Leave Freedom's ark on loftier heights.

ABRAHAM LINCOLN

Richard Henry Stoddard

THIS man whose homely face you look upon
Was one of Nature's masterful, great men;
Born with strong arms, that unfought battles won,
Direct of speech and cunning with the pen.
Chosen for large designs, he had the art
Of winning with his humor, and he went
Straight to his mark, which was the human heart;
Wise, too, for what he could not break he bent.

THE PRAISE OF LINCOLN

Upon his back a more than Atlas-load,
The burden of the Commonwealth, was laid;
He stooped, and rose up to it, though the road
Shot suddenly downward, not a whit dismayed:
    Patiently resolute, what the stern hour
    Demanded, that he was,—that Man, that Power.

THE NIGHT RIDE OF ANCIENT ABE

Miles O'Reilly

(Charles Graham Halpine)

Not a drum was heard, not a party cry—
    We were all most terribly flurried,
As, with kindling horror in heart and eye,
    Old Abe to the rail-cars we hurried.

We hurried him quickly, at dead of night,
    A disguise o'er his long limbs throwing,
By the struggling moonbeam's misty light,
    And a bull's-eye dimly glowing.

No useless pageant or pomp we had,
    But with Sumner's cloak around him,
And canny Sim Cameron's cap of plaid
    To put through in the dark we bound him.

Few and short were the words he said,
    As we looked in his face of sorrow,
But sadly we thought of the row to be made
    In the *Herald* and *Times* of the morrow.

THE PRAISE OF LINCOLN

We thought, as we jostled him into the car
  Without either cheer or ovation,
What a laugh there would be when the news spread
    afar
  Of the Rail-splitter's ass-ass-ination.

We started the train, and the hero was off,
  Evading each Plug-Ugly sentry;
But, Lord! how the heathen will guffaw and scoff
  At this new kind of "national entry."

Gayly the *Post* of the plot may make light,
  And talk of the "Tooley street tailors,"
But, snugly installed in the mansion of white,
  The Rail-splitter laughs at all railers.

THE ANCIENT ABE

Miles O'Reilly

(Charles Graham Halpine)

(*Air: "The Shan Van Vocht"*)

"LET us up and do or die,"
  Says the Ancient Abe;
"Let us up and do or die,"
  Says old Abe;
"We will rear our banner high
As the stars are in the sky,
And our enemies shall fly,"
  Says the ancient Abe.

Then to Washington he flew,
  Did the ancient Abe—
Then to Washington he flew,
  Did old Abe;

THE PRAISE OF LINCOLN

'And he swore by black and blue
All seceders to "put through,"
And the forts to man anew,
  Did the ancient Abe.

Has he kept his solemn vow,
  Has the ancient Abe?
Has he kept his solemn vow,
  Has old Abe?
By the Lord! we see him bow
At the shadow of a row—
'Tis an ugly case of "cow"
  With the ancient Abe.

For without a cannon fired
  By the ancient Abe—
Not a gun or cracker fired
  By old Abe—
He has peacefully retired,
Granting all the South desired,
Sinking down as it aspired,
  Has the ancient Abe.

"Major Anderson's to blame,"
  Cries the ancient Abe;
"It is he that is to blame,"
  Says old Abe;
And thus to hide the shame
Of a heart that is not "game,"
He befouls that honored name,
  Does the ancient Abe.

Oh, my friends, we've had enough
  Of this ancient Abe—
Much more than was enough
  Of old Abe;

THE PRAISE OF LINCOLN

He is made of such weak stuff,
The South beats his game of bluff,
And I fear they'll ride him rough—
    Ride the ancient Abe.

Let us watch and wait and pray
    For the ancient Abe—
For our country let us pray,
    And for Abe;
Let us help him if we may,
When he falters on the way,
Guide him back when gone astray.—
    Poor bewildered Abe.

For though all the saddest fates
    Link with ancient Abe—
All the most despairing fates
    Link with Abe—
He is captain in the gates
Of these grand United States,
And must be till time abates—
    Hapless ancient Abe.

Let us therefore, though we squirm
    Under ancient Abe—
Though we writhe and groan and squirm
    Under Abe—
Let us all stand true and firm,
Of his courage nurse the germ,
And in patience bear the term
    Of the ancient Abe.

ABRAHAM LINCOLN—1863

Richard Realf

I

It touches to the quick the spirit of one
  Who knows what Freedom is; whose eyes have seen
The crops thou sowest ripen in the sun;
  Whose feet have trod the fields wherein men glean
The harvests of thy lonely hours, when thou
  Didst grapple with the Incarnate Insolence
  Lording the Land with impious pretense,
And very bravely on its arrogant brow
  Didst set thy sealed abhorrence—when he hears
The glib invectives which men launch at thee,
  Beloved of Peoples, crowned in all thy years
Nestor of all our chiefs of Liberty,
  As if thou wert some devil of crafty spell
  Let loose to lure the unwary unto hell.

II

But thou art wiser; thy clear spiritual sense
  Threading our tangled darkness, seest how
The equilibriums of Omnipotence
  Poise the big worlds in safety. Disavow
And jeer thee as men will, stab, howl, and curse,
  Nor pluck the noble memories of thy name
From the glad keeping of the Universe
  Quickened with the conjunction of thy spirit,
For lo! thou art Ours alone—and yet thou art
  Nature's, Mankind's, the Age's! We inherit
Joint treasures from thee; but we stand apart
  From all the earth in bitter trespasses
  'Gainst thee and thy great throb of tenderness.

III

Nathless, let not our cold ingratitude
  Make sad the soul within thee: in the years
When the full meanings of our brotherhood
  Roll their high revelations round the spheres,
The solemn passion of thy life shall be
  A wonder and a worship unto all,
  Whose eyes behold the Apocalyptical
Transfiguration of Humanity.
  Meanwhile, because thy recompense is pain,
Weary not thou; invisible lips shall kiss
  The trouble from thy heart and from thy brain,
In all the days of thy self-sacrifice,
  Thy blessed hurts being still thy amplest wage,
  Thou Archimedes of Love's leverage.

LINCOLN—1865

Lewis V. F. Randolph

What hast thou hidden, mournful Night!
  What have ye seen, O Stars!
A country turning to the Light,
  Covered with sacred scars,
Plunged back in dark and dire distress
  By one foul, fiendish deed
That leaves a people comfortless—
  Makes every true heart bleed.

It was no common crime that struck
  That God-like man to earth—
Ruthless, the tender eye to pluck
  That watched our land's new birth.

THE PRAISE OF LINCOLN

No word—nor Treason, Fratricide,
   Nor Parricide—can tell
His act, whose hand was so allied
   With powers of deepest hell.

This was our brother, father—more;—
   Chosen by mother-land,
His name her valiant sons adore
   In every patriot band.
God of our brethren and our sires!
   Be Thou our Father now;
Whilst at our altars and our fires
   In prayerful grief we bow!

ABRAHAM LINCOLN

Frank Moore

(January 1st, 1863)

STAND like an anvil, when 'tis beaten
   With the full vigor of the smith's right arm!
Stand like the noble oak-tree, when 'tis eaten
   By Saperda and his ravenous swarm!
For many smiths will strike the ringing blows
Ere the red drama now enacting close;
And human insects, gnawing at thy fame,
Conspire to bring thy honored head to shame.

Stand like the firmament, upholden
   By an invisible but Almighty hand!
He whomsoever *Justice* doth embolden,
   Unshaken, unseduced, unawed shall stand.
Invisible support is mightier far,
With noble aims than walls of granite are;
And simple consciousness of justice gives
Strength to a purpose while that purpose lives.

169

Stand like the rock that looks defiant
  Far o'er the surging seas that lash its form!
Composed, determined, watchful, self-reliant,
  Be master of thyself, and rule the storm!
And thou shalt soon behold the bow of peace
Span the broad heavens, and the wild tumult cease;
And see the billows, with the clouds that meet,
Subdued and calm, come crouching to thy feet.

ABRAHAM LINCOLN'S CHRISTMAS GIFT

Nora Perry

'Twas in eighteen hundred and sixty-four,
That terrible year when the shock and roar
Of the nation's battles shook the land,
And the fire leapt up into fury fanned,

The passionate, patriotic fire,
With its throbbing pulse and its wild desire
To conquer and win, or conquer and die,
In the thick of the fight when hearts beat high

With the hero's thrill to do and to dare,
'Twixt the bullet's rush and the muttered prayer.
In the North, and the East and the great Northwest,
Men waited and watched with eager zest

For news of the desperate, terrible strife,—
For a nation's death or a nation's life;
While over the wires there flying sped
News of the wounded, the dying and dead.

THE PRAISE OF LINCOLN

"Defeat and defeat! Ah! what was the fault
Of the grand old army's sturdy assault
At Richmond's gates?" in querulous key
Men questioned at last impatiently,

As the hours crept by, and day by day
They watched the Potomac Army at bay.
Defeat and defeat! It was here, just here,
In the very height of the fret and fear,

Click, click! across the electric wire
Came suddenly flashing words of fire,
And a great shout broke from city and town
At the news of Sherman's marching down,—

Marching down on his way to the sea
Through the Georgia swamps to victory.
Faster and faster the great news came,
Flashing along like tongues of flame,—

McAllister ours! And then, ah! then,
To that patientest, tenderest, noblest of men,
This message from Sherman came flying swift,—
"I send you Savannah for a Christmas gift!"

HUSHED BE THE CAMPS TO-DAY

Walt Whitman

(May 4th, 1865)

HUSHED be the camps to-day,
And soldiers, let us drape our war-worn weapons,
And each with musing soul retire to celebrate
Our dear commander's death.

No more for him life's stormy conflicts,
Nor victory, nor defeat—no more time's dark events,
Charging like ceaseless clouds across the sky.

But sing, poet, in our name.
Sing of the love we bore him—because you, dweller in
    camps, know it truly.

As they invault the coffin there,
Sing—as they close the doors of earth upon him—one
    verse
For the heavy hearts of soldiers.

CROWN HIS BLOOD-STAINED PILLOW

Julia Ward Howe

CROWN his blood-stained pillow
  With a victor's palm;
Life's receding billow
  Leaves eternal calm.

At the feet Almighty
  Lay this gift sincere;
Of a purpose weighty,
  And a record clear.

With deliverance freighted
  Was this passive hand,
And this heart, high-fated,
  Would with love command.

Let him rest serenely
  In a Nation's care,
Where her waters queenly
  Make the West more fair.

172

THE PRAISE OF LINCOLN

In the greenest meadow
  That the prairies show,
Let his marble shadow
  Give all men to know:

"Our First Hero, living,
  Made his country free;
Heed the Second's giving,
  Death for Liberty."

THE PRESIDENT'S PROCLAMATION

Howard Glyndon

(Laura C. Redden Searing)

Authorizing the Mustering Into Service of Colored Regiments

LIFT up the bowed, desponding head,
  O long-enduring race!
Let the meek sufferance of your eyes
  Abash the tyrant's face.

Take courage, O despairing race!
  The tides of fortune turn,
When white men take in kindly clasp
  The hands they used to spurn!

Go into battle side by side
  With men of fairer hue;
We will not hinder by our scorn
  The work you have to do!

Despised, rejected, cast away,
  Ye are God's children yet!
And on the foreheads of your race
  His mercy-seal is set!

173

LINCOLN CENTENARY ODE

Percy Mackaye

I

No ceremonial
Of pealèd chime was there, or blarèd horn,
Such as hath blazoned births of lesser kings,
When he—the elder brother of us all,
Lincoln—was born.
At his nativity
Want stood as sponsor, stark Obscurity
Was midwife, and all lonely things
Of nature were unconscious ministers
To endow his spirit meek
With their own melancholy. So when he—
An infant king of commoners—
Lay in his mother's arms, of all the earth
(Which now his fame wears for a diadem)
None heeded of his birth;
Only a star burned over Bethlehem
More bright, and, big with prophecy,
A secret gust from that far February
Fills now the organ-reeds that peal his centenary.

II

Who shall distil in song those epic years?
Only the Sibyl of simplicity,
Touched by the light and dew of common tears,
Might chant that homely native Odyssea.

For there are lives too large in simple truth
For art to limn or elegy to gauge,
And there are men so near to God's own ruth
They are the better angels of their age,

174

THE PRAISE OF LINCOLN

And such was he: beyond the pale of song
His grandeur looms in truth, with awful grace;
He lives where beauty's origins belong
Deep in the primal raptures of his race.

Yet may we strive to trace
His shadow—where it pulses vast
Upon imagination, cast
By the oft-handtrimm'd lamp of history—
In carved breath, or bronze, that we might scan
The imagined child and man
Whose life and death are looms of our own destiny.

III

.   .   .   .

How like a saga of the northern sea
Our own Kentucky hero-tale begins!
    Once on a time, far in a wintry wood,
    A lone hut stood;
    There lived a poor man's son that was to be
    A master man of earth.
And so for us,
Like children in the great hall of his spirit,
The homebred fairy-story spins
Annals whose grace the after-times inherit.

The uncouth homestead by the trail of Boone,
The untitled grant, the needy exodus,
The ox-cart on the Indiana heath,
The log shack by the Sangamon, and soon
The fever'd mother and the forest death—
From these the lonely epic wanders on.

The longshank boy, with visage creased by toil
And laughter of the soil,

175

Cribbing his book of statutes from his chore,
Erelong his nooning fellows of the field
Hail their scrub-orator, or at sundown—
Slouching his gaunt and sallow six-foot-four—
Their native Touchstone of the village store.
Or from the turf, where he has matched his build
To throw the county champion in the loam,
Idly he saunters home
To rock some mother's cradle in the town;
Or, stretched on counter calico, with Clay
And organ-sounding Webster, dream the night away.

But time begins
Slowly to sift the substance from the slag.
And now along the county pike's last lap,
With giant shins
Shut knifewise in his wabbling rattletrap,
The circuit lawyer trots his tired nag
Toward the noon tavern, reins up, and unrolls
His awkward length of wrinkled bombazine,
Clutching his tattered green
Umbrella and thin carpetsack,
And flings a joke that makes the rafters roar:
As if, uplooming from of yore,
Some quaint-accoutered king of trolls,
Out-elbowing a sexton's suit of black
In Christmas glee,
Should sudden crack
His shrilly jest of shrewd hilarity,
And shake the clambering urchins from his back.

IV

How vast the war invisible
When public weal battles with public will!
Proudly the stars of Union hung their wreath
On the young nation's lordly architrave;

THE PRAISE OF LINCOLN

Yet underneath
Its girding vaults and groins,
Half the fair fabric rested on the loins
And stooping sinews of a slave,
That—raised to the just stature of a man—
Should rend the whole asunder.
And now the million-headed serf began
To stir in wonder,
And from the land, appalled by that low thunder,
"Kansas-Nebraska!" rang
The cry, and with exceeding pang
Out of the earth blood sprang
And out of men's hearts, fire.   And that hot flame,
Fed by the book that burned in all men's homes,
Kindled from horizon to horizon
Anguish and shame
And aspiration, by its glow
Ruddying the state-house domes
With monstrous shadows of Dred Scott
And gaunt-limbed effigies of Garrison.

Then in the destined man matured the slow
Strong grandeur of that lot
Which singled him; till soon,
Ushered with lordly train,
The champion Douglas met him on the plain,
And the broad prairie moon
Peered through white schooners at the mad bonfires
And multitudes astir,
Where—roped like wrestlers in a ring—
The *Little Giant* faced the *Railsplitter;*
And serious crowds harked silently,
With smothered taunts and ires,
While Commonsense grappled with "Sovereignty,"
Till the lank, long-armed wrestler made his fling.
And still sublime

With common sympathy, that cool
Sane manfulness survives: *You can not fool*
All of the people all the time.
No; by that power we misname fate,
'Tis character which molds the state.
Statutes are dead when men's ideals dissent,
And public will is more than precedent,
And manhood more than constitutions can create.
Higher than bar and documental ban,
Men's highest court is still the heart of Man.

v

Bold to his country, sick with compromise,
Spoke the plain advocate;
Half slave, half free, our Union dies,
But it shall live! And done with sophistries,
The people answered with tempestuous call
That shook the revolutionary dead,
And high on rude rails garlanded
Bore their backwoodsman to the Capitol.
"Who is this common huckster?" sneered the great,
"This upstart Solon of the Sangamon?"
And chastened Douglas answered: "He is one
Who wrestles well for Truth." But some
Scowled unbelief, and some smiled bitterly;
And so, beneath the derrick'd half-built dome,
While dumb artillery
And guards battalioned the black lonely form,
He took his oath.
We are not enemies, but friends!
Yet scarce the sad rogation ends
Ere the warped planks of Union split in storm
Of dark secession.

THE PRAISE OF LINCOLN

　　　　　Then, as on a raft
Flood-rended, where by night the Ohio sweeps
Into the Mississippi, 'mid the roil
Of roaring waters with eroded soil
From hills primeval, the strong poleman keeps
Silence, midway the shallows and the rocks,
To steer his shipment safe, while fore and aft
The scrambling logmen scream at him, or scold
With prayers and malisons, or burst the locks
And loot the precious bales, so—deaf and mute
To sneers and imprecations both—
The lone Flatboatman of the Union poled
His country's wreck midstream, and resolute
Held still his goal:
To lash his ballast to the sundered half,
And save the whole.

"They seek a sign,
But no sign shall be given them," he said;
And reaching Godward, with his pilot's gaff
Probed in the dark, among the drowning and the dead,
And sunk his plummet line
Deep in the people's heart, where still his own heart
　　　bled,
And fathomed there the inundated shore
Swept by the flood and storm of elemental war.

．　　．　　．　　．　　．　　．　　．

IX

The loving and the wise
May seek—but seek in vain—to analyze
The individual man, for having caught
The mystic clue of thought,

179

Sudden they meet the controverting whim,
And fumbling with the enchanted key,
Lose it then utterly.
Æsop and old Isaiah held in him
Strange sessions, winked at by Artemus Ward,
Till sudden in their midst bright Seraphim
Stood, summoned by a sad, primeval bard
Who, bearing still no name, has ever borne
Within his heart the music of mankind:
Sometime a lonely singer blind
Beside the Ionian sea;
Sometime, between two thieves in scorn,
A face in Calvary.

That was his master soul—
The mystic demi-god of common man—
Who, templed in the steadfast mind,
Hid his shy gold of genius in the bran
Of Hoosier speech and garb, softening the wan
Strong face of shrewdness with strange aureole.

He was the madstone to his country's ire,
Drawing the rancorous blood of envious quarrel
Alike from foe and friend; his pity, stirr'd,
Restored to its bough the storm-unnested bird,
Or raised the wallow'd pig from out the mire.
And he who sowed in sweat his boyhood's crop,
And tackled Euclid with a wooden spade,
And excavated Blackstone from a barrel
To hold moot trials in the gloaming, made
By lighted shavings in a cooper's shop,
He is the people's still—their Railsplitter,
Himself a rail, clean-grained, of character
Self-hewn in the dark glades of Circumstance

THE PRAISE OF LINCOLN

From that deep-hearted tree
Democracy,
Which, by our race's heritage,
Reforests age on age,
Perpetual in strong fecundity.

   .   .   .   .

XI

But he is more than ours, as we are more
Than yet the world dares dream.   His stature grows
With that illimitable state
Whose sovereignty ordains no tribute shore
And borderland of hate,
But grounds its justice in the joy it sows.
His spirit is still a power to emancipate
Bondage—more base, being more insidious,
Than serfdom—that cries out in the midst of us
For virtue, born of opportunity,
And manhood, weighed in honest human worth,
And freedom, based in labor. He stands forth
'Mongst nations old—a new-world Abraham,
The patriarch of peoples still to be,
Blending all visions of the promised land
In one Apocalypse.

          His voice is heard—
Thrilling the molder'd lintels of the past—
In Asia; old Thibet is stirred
With warm imaginings;
Ancestral China, 'midst her mysteries,
Unmasks, and flings
Her veils wide to the Occident; the wand
Of hope awakes prone Hierapolis;
Even by the straits of old that Io swam,
The immemorial sultan, scepterless,
Stands awed; and heartened by that bold success,
Pale Russia rises from her holocaust.

And still the emancipating influence,
The secret power, the increasing truth, are his,
For they are ours: ours by the potencies
Poured in our nation from the founts of time,
Blending in us the mystic seeds of men,
To sow them forth again
For harvests more sublime
Throughout the world.

XII

Leave, then, that wonted grief
Which honorably mourns its martyred dead,
And newly hail instead
The birth of him, our hardy shepherd chief,
Who by green paths of old democracy
Leads still his tribes to uplands of glad peace.

As long as—out of blood and passion blind—
Springs the pure justice of the reasoning mind,
And justice, bending, scorns not to obey
Pity, that once in a poor manger lay,
As long as, thrall'd by time's imperious will,
Brother hath bitter need of brother, still
His presence shall not cease
To lift the ages toward his human excellence,
And races yet to be
Shall in a rude hut do him reverence
And solemnize a simple man's nativity.

ABRAHAM LINCOLN

Joel Benton

SOME opulent force of genius, soul, and race,
  Some deep life-current from far centuries
  Flowed to his mind, and lighted his sad eyes,
And gave his name, among great names, high place.

182

THE PRAISE OF LINCOLN

But these are miracles we may not trace—
   Nor say why from a source and lineage mean
   He rose to grandeur never dreamt or seen,
Or told on the long scroll of history's space.
The tragic fate of one broad hemisphere
   Fell on stern days to his supreme control,
All that the world and liberty held dear
   Pressed like a nightmare on his patient soul.
Martyr beloved, on whom, when life was done,
Fame looked, and saw another Washington!

ABRAHAM LINCOLN

Samuel Francis Smith

HEROIC statesman, hail!
   Thy honored name,
With instrument and song, we laud,
   And poet's lays;
How every mountain top, and sheltered rail,
   And rock and stream,
And lisping tongue of infancy and age,
   And manhood's prime and woman's love,
   Combine thy honored name to praise.

   As to Anchises' tomb,
With reverent love, pious Æneas came,
   Intent, with festal rites
   To crown his father's fame,—
So we, with grateful reverence, come to pay
This loving tribute at the sacred shrine,
   The statesman wise, the martyr prince,
     The peerless man,
And on his tomb our fragrant garlands lay.

Like the wild eagle's flight,
When from his rocky height,
Down on the plain he swoops, free as the air,—
Born with a soul of fire,
Born to be free,
Patient in toil, and danger, and alarm,
He ventured all for love of liberty,
And helped the lowly in that bliss to share.
Grandly he loved and lived;
Not his own age alone
Bears the proud impress of his sovereign mind.
Down the long march of history,
Ages and men shall see
What one great soul can be,
What one great soul can do,
To make a nation true,—
To raise the weak,
The lost to seek,
To be a ruler and a father too;
No scheming tool,
No slave to godless rule,
Gracious, efficient, meek, sublime, refined.

Ambitious,—not of wealth,
Nor power, nor place;
His aim, a nobler race;
His title eminent,—An honest man.
His, to lift up the rude;
His, to be great as good,
And good as great;
His, to stem error's flood;
His, but to help and bless;
His to work righteousness,
And save the state.

THE PRAISE OF LINCOLN

Brave, self-reliant, wise,
Calm in emergencies,
Steady, alike, to wait, and prompt to move;
In counsel, great and safe;
Prudent to plan;
Righteous to deal with sin;
Prone, less to force than win;
Strong in his own stern will, and strong in God;
Conquering, alone, to bless,—
A loving man.

Firm, but yet merciful;
In pity bountiful;
Calmly considerate, serenely just;
Nobly forgiving to the fallen foe,—
He, the meek sufferer from Oppression's blow,
Repaying ill with good,
E'en as the sandal-wood
Bathes with rare perfume the sharp axe that smites;
Unflinching for the right,
Whate'er might come,
And, until death,
Fervent, decided, faithful to his trust.

Great souls can never die:
Death and decay's damp fingers
Waste but the mortal;
A noble life spreads its fair vista wide.
Beyond death's portal,
Like an unfading light
The life work lingers.
The hero dies; statesman and soldier fall;
The nation finds new life,
And prosperous years, and wealth, and peace,
And hearts at rest, and grander aims,
And righteousness,

And souls that dare to be,
Just as God made them,—free;
And he who falls, crushed in the bitter strife,
Lives magnified, exalted, ever lives;
His work bears fruit immortal.

So the great sun, majestic, plows his way
Through clouds, and storms, and dim eclipse,
And winter's cold and summer's heat;
And, nightly, dips
His flaming disc in the broad western sea,
But scatters light and blessing all the day.
Setting, he leaves the world
Richer and better for his light and love;
Warmer, more fertile, more benign;
Sets, but to rise, on other lands, and shine
For ever, in the galaxy divine.

ABRAHAM LINCOLN

Edmund Clarence Stedman

(Assassinated Good Friday, 1865)

"FORGIVE them, for they know not what they do!"
He said, and so went shriven to his fate,—
Unknowing went, that generous heart and true.
Even while he spoke the slayer lay in wait,
And when the morning opened Heaven's gate
There passed the whitest soul a nation knew.
Henceforth all thoughts of pardon are too late;
They, in whose cause that arm its weapon drew,
Have murdered Mercy. Now alone shall stand
Blind Justice, with the sword unsheathed she wore.
Hark, from the Eastern to the Western strand,
The swelling thunder of the people's roar:
What words they murmur,—Fetter not her hand!
So let it smite, such deeds shall be no more!

WHEN LINCOLN DIED

Edward William Thomson

Already Appomattox day
Seemed to our hearts an age away,
Although the April-blossomed trees
Were droning with the very bees
That bumbled round the conference
When Lee resigned his long defense,
And Grant's new gentleness subdued
The iron Southern fortitude.

From smoldering leaves the smoky smell
Wreathed round Virginian fields a spell
Of homely aromatic haze,
So like New Hampshire springtime days
About the slopes of Moosilauke
It numbed my homesick heart to talk,
And when the bobolinks trilled "Rejoice!"
My comrade could not trust his voice.

We were two cavalrymen assigned
To safeguard Pinckney womankind,
Whose darkies rambled Lord knows where
In some persuasion that they were
Thenceforth, in ease, at public charge
To live as gentlemen at large—
A purpose which, they'd heard, the war
Was made by "Massa Linkum" for.

The pillared mansion, battle-wrecked,
Yet stood with ivied front erect,
Its mossy gables, shell-fire-torn,
Were still in lordliness upborne
Above the neighboring barns, well stored
With war-time's rich tobacco hoard;

THE PRAISE OF LINCOLN

But on the place for food, was nought
Save what our commissary brought
To keep the planter's folk alive
Till Colonel Pinckney might arrive
Paroled from northward, if his head
Lay not among the prisoner dead.

We'd captured him ten days before,
When Richard Ewell's veteran corps,
Half-naked, starving, fought amain
To save their dwindling wagon-train.
Since they were weak and we were strong,
The battle was not overlong.
Again I see the prisoners stare
Exultant at the orange glare
Of sunlit flame they saw aspire
Up from the train they gave to fire.
They'd shred apart their hero flags
To share the silk as heart-worn rags.
The trampled field was strewn about
With wreckage of the closing rout—
Their dead, their wounded, rifles broke,
Their mules and horses slain in yoke;
Their torn-up records, widely spread,
Fluttered around the muddy dead—
So bitter did their hearts condemn
To ruin all we took with them.

Ten days before! The war was past,
The Union saved, Peace come at last,
And Father Abraham's words of balm
Gentling the war-worn States to calm.
Of all the miracles he wrought
That was the sweetest. Men who'd fought
So long they'd learned to think in hate,
And savor blood when bread they ate,

188

THE PRAISE OF LINCOLN

And hear their buried comrades wail,
How long, O Lord, doth wrong prevail?

List'ning alike, in blue or gray,
Felt war's wild passions soothed away.
By homely touches in the air
That morning was so sweet and rare
That Father Abraham's soul serene
Seemed brooding over all the scene;
And when we found the plow, I guess
We were so tired of idleness
Our farmer fingers yearned to hold
The handles, and to sense the mould
Turning the earth behind the knife.

Jim gladdened as with freshened life;—
"Say, John," said he, "I'm feeling beat
To know what these good folks will eat
When you and I are gone. Next fall
They're sure to have no crop at all.
All their tobacco's confiscate
By Washington—and what a state
Of poverty they're bound to see!
Say, buddy, what if you and me
Just hitch our cavalry horses now
Up to this blamed Virginia plow,
And run some furrows through the field?
With commissary seed they'd yield
A reasonable crop of corn."
"They will," said I, "as sure's you're born!"

Quickly we rigged, with rope and straps
And saddle leathers—well, perhaps
The Yankiest harness ever planned
To haul a plow through farming land.
It made us kind of happy, too,
Feeling like Father Abraham knew.

THE PRAISE OF LINCOLN

The Pinckney place stood on a rise,
And when we'd turned an end, our eyes
Would see the mansion war had wrecked,—
Such desolation! I suspect
The women's hearts were mourning sore;
But not one tear we saw—they bore
Composed the fortune fate had sent—
But, O dear Lord, how still they went!
I've seen such quiet in a shroud,
Inscrutably resigned and proud.

Yet, when we'd worked an hour or two,
And plain was what we meant to do,
Mother and daughters came kind-eyed,—
"Soldiers—my soldier husband's pride
Will be to thank you well—till then
We call you friendly, helpful men—"
It seemed she stopped for fear of tears.
She turned—they went—Oh, long the years
Gone by since that brave lady spoke—
And yet I hear the voice that broke.

We watched them climb the lilac hill,
Again the spring grew strangely still
Ere, far upon the turnpike road,
Across a clattering bridge, where flowed
Through sand the stream of Pinckney Run,
We heard the galloping of one
Who, hidden by the higher ground,
Pounded as fast as horse could pound.
Then—all again was still as death—
Till up the slope with laboring breath,
A white steed rose—his rider gray
Spurring like mad his staggering way.

THE PRAISE OF LINCOLN

The man was old and tall and white,
His glooming eyes looked dead to light,
He rode with such a fateful air
I felt a coldness thrill my hair,
He rode as one hard hit rides out
In horror from some battle rout,
Bearing a cry for instant aid—
That aspect made my heart afraid.
The death-like rider drew no rein,
Nor seemed to note us on the plain,
Nor seemed to know how weak in stride
His horse strove up the long hillside;
When down it lurched, on foot the man
Up through the fringing lilacs ran,
His left hand clutching empty air
As if his saber still hung there.

'Twas plain as day that human blast
Was Colonel Pinckney home at last,
And we were free, since ordered so
That with his coming we might go;
Yet on we plowed—the sun swung high,
Quiet the earth and blue the sky—
Silent we wrought, as men who wait
Some half-imagined stroke of fate,
While through the trembling shine came knells
Tolling from far-off Lynchburg bells.

The solemn, thrilling sounds of gloom
Bore portents of tremendous doom,
On smoky zephyrs drifted by
Shadows of hosts in charging cry,
In fields where silence ruled profound
Growling musketry echoed round,
Pale phantom ranks did starkly pass
Invisible across the grass,

Flags ghosted wild in powder fume
Till, miracled in memory's room,
Rang the old regiment's rousing cheer
For Father Abraham, smiling queer.

'Twas when we turned a furrow's end
We saw a martial form descend
From Mansion Hill the lilac way,
Till in our field the veteran gray
Stood tall and straight as at parade,
And yet as one with soul dismayed.
That living emblem of the South
Faced us unblenching, though his mouth
So quivered with the spoken word
It seemed a tortured heart we heard;—
"Soldiers"—he eyed us nobly when
We stood to "attention"—"Soldiers—men,
For this good work my thanks are due—
But—men—O God—men, if you knew,
Your kindly hands had shunned the plow—
For hell comes up between us now!—
Oh, sweet was peace—but gone is peace—
Murder and hate have fresh release!—
The deed be on the assassin's head!—
Men—*Abraham Lincoln's lying dead!"*

He steadied then—he told us through
All of the tale that Lynchburg knew,
While dumbly raged my anguished heart
With woe from pity wrenched apart,
For, in the fresh red furrow, bled
'Twixt us and him the martyred dead.
That precious crimson ran so fast
It merged in tinge with battles past,—
Hatcher's, Five Forks, The Wilderness,
The Bloody Angle's maddened stress;

THE PRAISE OF LINCOLN

Down Cemetery Hill there poured
Torrents that stormed to Kelly's Ford,
And twice Manassas flung its flood
To swell the four years' tide of blood,
And Sumter blazed, and Ellsworth fell,
While memory flashed its gleams of hell.

The colonel's staring eyes declared
In visions wild as ours he shared,
Until—dear Christ—with Thine was blent
The death-transfigured President.
Strange—*strange*—the crown of thorns he wore,
His outspread hands were pierced sore,
And down his old black coat a tide
Flowed from the javelin-wounded side;
Yet 'twas his homely self there stood,
And gently smiled across the blood,
And changed the mystic stream to tears
That swept afar the angry years,
And flung me down as falls a child
Whose heart breaks out in weeping wild.

.   .   .   .   .   .

Yet in that field we plowed no more,
We shunned the open Southern door,
We saddled up, we rode away,—
'Tis that that troubles me to-day.

Full thirty years to dust were turned
Before my pondering soul had learned
The blended vision there was sent
In sign that our Belovèd meant;—
Children who wrought so mild my will,
Plow the long furrow kindly still,
'Tis sweet the Father's work to see
Done for the memory of me.

THE DEAD PRESIDENT

Edward Rowland Sill

WERE there no crowns on earth,
No evergreen to wreathe a hero wreath,
That he must pass beyond the gates of death,
Our hero, our slain hero, to be crowned?
Could there on our unworthy earth be found
　　　Naught to befit his worth?

　　　The noblest soul of all!
When was there ever since our Washington,
A man so pure, so wise, so patient—one
Who walked with this high good alone in sight,
To speak, to do, to sanction only Right,
　　　Though very heaven should fall.

　　　Ah, not for him we weep;
What honor more could be in store for him?
Who would have had him linger in our dim
And troublesome world, when his great work was
　　done—
Who would not leave that worn and weary one
　　　Gladly to sleep?

　　　For us the stroke was just;
We were not worthy of that patient heart;
We might have helped him more, not stood apart,
And coldly criticised his works and ways—
Too late now, all too late—our little praise
　　　Sounds hollow o'er his dust.

　　　Be merciful, O our God!
Forgive the meanness of our human hearts,
That never, till a noble soul departs,
See half the worth, or hear the angel's wings
Till they go rustling heavenward as he springs
　　　Up from the mounded sod.

194

THE PRAISE OF LINCOLN

Yet what a deathless crown
Of Northern pine and Southern orange-flower,
For victory, and the land's new bridal-hour,
Would we have wreathed for that beloved brow!
Sadly upon his sleeping forehead now
We lay our cypress down.

O martyred one, farewell!
Thou hast not left thy people quite alone,
Out of thy beautiful life there comes a tone
Of power, of love, of trust, a prophecy,
Whose fair fulfilment all the earth shall be,
And all the Future tell.

ABRAHAM LINCOLN

William Henry Venable

(1864)

No adulation vain the poet brings,
  Investing thee with godlike excellence;
In eloquence of truth he fitly sings
  Thy eulogy by praising Common Sense,
Firm Honesty and Courage undismayed,
  Deep Faith and Magnanimity sublime!
What though the violent thy name upbraid?
  Thy Wisdom's vindication leave to Time.
O man of Fate, abide the sure event;
  Writ in the stars, behold the just decree!
The God of Love chose thee His instrument,
  To save the Union, set the Bondman free!
Smile on amid thy care, for even now
  The war-cloud scatters and its thunders cease;
A grateful Nation waits to crown thy brow
  With healing leaves of victory and peace.

195

THE LINCOLN-CHILD

James Oppenheim

CLEARING in the forest,
In the wild Kentucky forest,
And the stars, wintry stars strewn above!
O Night that is the starriest
Since Earth began to roll—
For a Soul
Is born out of Love!
Mother love, father love, love of Eternal God—
Stars have pushed aside to let him through—
Through heaven's sun-sown deeps
One sparkling ray of God
Strikes the clod—
(And while an angel-host through wood and clearing
      sweeps!)
Born in the Wild
The Child—
Naked, ruddy new,
Wakes with the piteous human cry and at the mother-
      heart sleeps.

To the mother wild berries and honey,
To the father awe without end,
To the child a swaddling of flannel—
And a dawn rolls sharp and sunny
And the skies of winter bend
To see the first sweet word penned
In the godliest human annal.

Frail Mother of the Wilderness—
How strange the world shines in
And the cabin becomes chapel
And the baby reveals God—

THE PRAISE OF LINCOLN

Sweet Mother of the Wilderness,
New worlds for you begin,
You have tasted of the apple
That giveth wisdom starred.

Do you dream, as all Mothers dream,
That the child at your heart
Is a marvel apart,
A frail star-beam
Unearthly splendid?
Ah, you are the one mother
Whose dream shall come true,
Though another, not you,
Shall see it ended.

Soon in the wide wilderness,
On a branch blown over a creek,
Up a trail of the wild 'coon,
In a lair of the wild bee,
The wildling boy, by Danger's stress,
Learnt the speech the wild things speak,
Learnt the Earth's eternal tune
Of God and starred Eternity—
Went to school where God Himself was master,
Went to church where Earth was minister—
And in Danger and Disaster
Felt his future manhood stir!

All about him lay the land,
Eastern cities, Western prairie,
Wild, immeasurable, grand,
But he was lost where blossomy boughs make airy
Bowers in the forest, and the sand
Makes brook-water a clear mirror that gives back
Green branches and trunks black
And clouds across the heavens lightly fanned.

Yet all the Future dreams, eager to waken,
Within that woodland soul—
And the bough of boy has only to be shaken
That the fruit drop whereby this Earth shall roll
A little nearer God than ever before.
Little recks he of war,
Of national millions waiting on his word—
Dreams still the Event unstirred
In the heart of the boy, the little babe of the wild—
But the years hurry and the tide of the sea
Of Time flows fast and ebbs, and he, even he,
Must leave the wilderness, the wood-haunts wild—
Soon shall the cyclone of Humanity
Tearing through Earth suck up this little child
And whirl him to the top, where he shall be
Riding the storm-column in the lightning-stroke,
Calm at the peak, while down below worlds rage,
And Earth goes out in blood and battle-smoke,
And leaves him with the sun—an epoch and an age!

Hushed be our hearts, and veneration
Steep us in joy,
Hushed be our mills, while a saved nation
Reveres this boy!
Hushed be our homes, while a holy elation
Makes the heart mild—
Each home has a child
And we worship a race of Lincolns in each that we
        love!
No, they may not stand above
The storm and steer the States,
These little children that are born from us—
No, they may not Lincolns prove
In the grandeur of their fates—
But Lincolns let them be in the heart and in the soul—
Even thus

THE PRAISE OF LINCOLN

Shall our Earth again toward God a little swifter,
    nearer roll,
Even thus
Shall our children touch the stars where we have only
    glimpsed the Goal.
Even thus and only thus
Through the Future's arch-like span
May they go American!
In his spirit shall they grow,
To his law they shall be bound,
With his light of God shall glow,
With his love of Man be crowned!

Think of the miracle!
A child so like our child,
A babe born in the wild,
A little clod of clay, sweet blossoming and beautiful,
Earth that is dumb and dead,
Earth risen in child-shape,
And suddenly agape
Are the eyes and lips, and spread
Is the heart and coiled the brain—
And lo, the Silences are slain—
In our Wilderness of Silence where we were only two,
Man and Wife,
Comes this third and like the voice of God breaks
    through
With his life—
And he answers back our Silence with his babbling,
    wordy strife—
Born of woman,
Born of man,
He is human
And he can
Grow beyond us in the grandeur we began!
And none greater than this boy

Whom this day
We revere with holy joy,
And we thank the stars the clay
In Kentucky took on human shape and spoke,
In the Wilderness awoke,
In the woodlands grew a creature of the wild,
This February child!

And lo, as he grew ugly, gaunt,
And gnarled his way into a man,
What wisdom came to feed his want,
What worlds came near to let him scan—
And as he fathomed through and through
Our dark and sorry human scheme,
He knew what Shakespeare never knew,
What Dante never dared to dream—
That Men are one
Beneath the sun,
And before God are equal souls—
This truth was his,
And this it is
That round him such a glory rolls—
For not alone he knew it as a truth,
He made it of his blood, and of his brain—
He crowned it on the day when piteous Booth
Sent a whole land to weeping with world-pain—
When a black cloud blotted the sun
And men stopped in the streets to sob,

To think Old Abe was dead—
Dead, and the day's work still undone,
Dead, and war's ruining heart athrob,
And earth with fields of carnage freshly spread—
Millions died fighting,
But in this man we mourned
Those millions, and one other—

THE PRAISE OF LINCOLN

And the States to-day uniting,
North and South,
East and West,
Speak with a people's mouth
A rhapsody of rest
To him our beloved best,
Our big, gaunt, homely brother—
Our huge Atlantic coast-storm in a shawl,
Our cyclone in a smile—our President,
Who knew and loved us all
With love more eloquent
Than his own words—with Love that in real deeds
    was spent.
Shelley's was a world of Love,
Carlyle's was a world of Work,
But Lincoln's was a world above
That of a dreamer or a clerk—
Lincoln wed the one to the other—
Made his a world where love gets into deeds—
Where man was more than merely brother,
Where the high Love was meeting human needs!
And lo, he made his plan
Memorably American!
Through all his life this mighty Faith unfurled!
O let us see, and let us know
That if our hearts could catch his glow
A faith like Lincoln's would transform the world!

Oh, to pour love through deeds—
To be as Lincoln was!—
That all the land might fill its daily needs
Glorified by a human Cause!
Then were America a vast World-Torch
Flaming a faith across the dying Earth,
Proclaiming from the Atlantic's rocky porch
That a New World was struggling at the Birth!

THE PRAISE OF LINCOLN

Ah, is this not the day
That rolls the Earth back to that mighty hour
When the sweet babe in the log-cabin lay
And God was in the room, a Presence and a Power?—
When all was sacred—even the father's heart—
And the stirred Wilderness stood still,
And roaring flume and shining hill
Felt the working of God's Will?
O living God, O Thou who living art,
And real, and near, draw, as at that babe's birth,
Into our souls and sanctify our Earth—

Let down Thy strength that we endure
Mighty and pure
As mothers and fathers of our own Lincoln-child—
Make us more wise, more true, more strong, more mild,
That we may day by day
Rear this wild blossom through its soft petals of clay,
That hour by hour
We may endow it with more human power
Than is our own—
That it may reach the goal
Our Lincoln long has shown!—
O Child—flesh of our flesh, bone of our bone,
Soul torn from out our Soul!
May you be great, and pure, and beautiful—
A Soul to search this world
To be a father, brother, comrade, son,
A toiler powerful,
A man with strength unfurled,
A man whose toil is done
One with God's Law above,
Work wrought through Love!

ABRAHAM LINCOLN

George Alfred Townsend

THE peaceful valley reaching wide,
   The wild war stilled on every hand;
On Pisgah's top our Prophet died,
   In sight of Promised Land.

A cheerful heart he bore alway,
   Though tragic years clashed on the while;
Death sat behind him at the play—
   His last look was a smile.

His single arm crushed wrong and thrall—
   That grand good will we only dreamed,
Two races weep around his pall,
   One saved and one redeemed.

No battle pike his march imbrued;
   Unarmed he went 'midst martial mails,
The footsore felt their strength renewed
   To hear his homely tales.

The trampled flag he raised again,
   And healed our eagle's broken wing;
The night that scattered armed men
   Saw scorpions rise to sting.

Down fell the brand in treason's hand
   Its gashes as he strove to stanch,
And o'er the waste of ruined land
   To take the Olive Branch.

The holy crest by murder stained,
   Upon its shattered portal lay;
The text this bravo's lips profaned
   Be sanctified for aye!

THE PRAISE OF LINCOLN

In still green field or belfried kirk,
  Where'er high boughs his sleep may lull,
Here closed his life, where closed his work,
  Beside the Capitol.

Be his no tomb perturbed and pent,
  With words too weak for grief begilt,—
Heap up his grander monument:
  The Union he rebuilt.

LINCOLN AND HIS PSALM

Benjamin F. Taylor

Move on, ye pilgrims, to the Springfield tomb—
Be proud to-day, O portico of gloom,
  Where lies the man in solitary state
    Who never caused a tear but when he died
      And set the flags around the world half mast.
  The gentle tribune and so grandly great
That e'en the utter avarice of Death
    That claims the world, and will not be denied,
Could only rob him of his mortal breath,
    How strange the splendor, though the man be past!
    His noblest inspiration was his last.
The statues of the Capitol are there
As when he stood upon the marble stair,
And said those words so tender, true, and just,
A royal psalm that took mankind on trust—
    Those words that will endure, and he in them
      While May wears flowers upon her broidered hem,
And all the marble snows and drifts to dust:
"Fondly do we hope, and fervently we pray
That this mighty scourge of war may speedily pass
      away;

THE PRAISE OF LINCOLN

With charity for all, with malice toward none,
  With firmness in the right
  As God shall give us light,
 Let us finish the work already begun—
Care for the battle sons, the Nation's wounds to bind,
Care for the helpless ones that they will leave behind,
Cherish it we will, achieve it if we can,
A just and lasting peace forever unto man!"

Amid old Europe's rude and thundering years
  When people strove as battle-clouds are driven,
One calm white angel of a day appears
  In every year a gift direct from Heaven,
Wherein from setting sun to setting sun
No thought or deed of bitterness was done.
"Day of the truce of God!" Be this day ours
  Until perpetual peace flows like a river,
And hopes as fragrant as the tribute flowers
  Fill all the land forever and forever.

ABRAHAM LINCOLN

Margaret E. Sangster

(February 12th, 1809—1909)

CHILD of the boundless prairie, son of the virgin soil,
Heir to the bearing of burdens, brother to them that
      toil;
God and Nature together shaped him to lead in the van,
In the stress of her wildest weather when the Nation
      needed a Man.

205

THE PRAISE OF LINCOLN

Eyes of a smoldering fire, heart of a lion at bay,
Patience to plan for to-morrow, valor to serve for to-
day,
Mournful and mirthful and tender, quick as a flash
with a jest,
Hiding with gibe and great laughter, the ache that was
dull in his breast!

Met were the Man and the Hour—Man who was
strong for the shock—
Fierce were the lightnings unleashed; in the midst, he
stood fast as a rock.
Comrade he was and commander he, who was meant
for the time,
Iron in council and action, simple, aloof, and sublime.

Swift slip the years from their tether, centuries pass
like a breath,
Only some lives are immortal, challenging darkness and
death.
Hewn from the stuff of the martyrs, write in the star-
dust his name,
Glowing, untarnished, transcendent, high on the records of Fame.

THE PEOPLE'S PRESIDENT

William Henry Venable

(April 14th and 15th, 1865)

I

REVERBERANT music of rejoicing bells
Loud heralded the morn, and cannon boomed,
And banners waved, and gladness woke the town.

THE PRAISE OF LINCOLN

As day rolled on, processions bearing high
Emblazoned emblems of fraternal love
Marched through the streets, their jubilant footsteps
      timed
To the accordant sound of martial horns,
To beat of drum and cymbal's joyous clang;
For armed rebellion vexed the States no more!
And all the day the pleasure-crested wave
Of thankful celebration swept along,
Then, self-exhausted, sunk and ebbed away,
To murmur on the formless coast of night,
Scarce heard save in the darkling caves of sleep.

A sudden clangor of alarum bells
At deep of midnight broke upon the air!
The household, out of slumber startling, rose,
To grope bewildered, till with trembling hand
They ope the door or lift the yielding sash,
Vague terror meanwhile shivering in their hearts,
And, thrusting fearful faces in the gloom,
They were aware of many sounds confused,
Uneasy questions, exclamations strange,
And flying rumors of appalling deeds.

A lowering cloud-rack overcast the sky,
And rueful winds went sobbing in the dark,
While tremulous upon the affrighted air
The tolling bells unceasingly proclaimed
Portentous tidings from the Capital,
Of tragic woe, and lamentation doled
For Lincoln dead,—the Gentle President,—
Untimely dead, by frantic murder slain!
Perpetual lamentation strangely joined
With raving threats of terrible revenge
And iron imprecations madly rung.

THE PRAISE OF LINCOLN

II

The morrow dawned. Through sad obscuring mists
Dimly the sun beheld a sorrowing world.
Once more the ways were thronged with citizens;
But music was not heard, nor any sound
Of song or laughter. None but children smiled,
And even children hushed their frolic mirth,
As comprehending vaguely some vast grief
That overshadowed all the stricken Land.

A dusky Freedman stood apart, alone;
His arms were folded and his head was bowed,
And in his isolate sorrow one might read
The utterless bereavement of a Race.

Old veterans their shaggy eyebrows knit,
And smote with vengeful foot the harmless earth,
Revealing inward wrath, and as they strode,
Their fingers' steely muscles would contract
As fain to clutch some deadly instrument
With fell design to render blood for blood.

A youthful hero, like forlorn Macduff,
Drew down his soldier cap to hide his tears,
And moaned a patriot anguish: "Would that I
Could yesternight have taken in my brain
That cruel ball, and so have shielded him."

And men recounted sadly every deed
Of him they mourned, and reperused his words,
Still pondering on his wisdom and his love,
And marveling that they had not sooner known
What prophet Soul unrecognized had dwelt
Among them, like the Nazarene, ofttimes
Like Him maligned, and crowned with envious thorns.

THE PRAISE OF LINCOLN

As woeful day moved wearily along,
Funereal emblems clouded every street;
Palatial hall and lowly cot obscure
Wore kindred black, and sable heraldry
Festooned each silken banner's drooping folds,
And fluttered sad by every tiny flag.

The sun went down; the people sought their homes;
And households sat in meditation deep,
Or spake of late events with grave surmise
Of dire mishaps and sorrows yet to come;
With doubts and fears and bitter questionings
Of providential justice.—But when night,
God's awful shadow, fell upon the town,
A holy calm fell also, and a trust
In the Omniscient Wisdom that ordains
All things by love divine, and reconciles
The distant issues of permitted wrong,
Unseen of men, still working final good.

ABRAHAM LINCOLN

P. C. Croll

(An Acrostic)

Akin to all that's noble, abreast with all that's grand,
Born to become the Savior of his imperiled land;
Reared 'mid such desperate hardships, his life bound to
        a cross,
A-treading out the vintage, restoring freedom's loss;
He was the greatest Champion of long down-trodden
        Right,
A Leader in the vanguard, a race's Dawn of Light—
Man with whom Truth was mightier than custom-for-
        tressed Might.

209

THE PRAISE OF LINCOLN

Lo! how he conquers drawbacks! Lo! obstacles all fall!
In moral mail-of-armor he fights at country's call,
Nor bows to fine-spun Error, nor fears well-buttressed
    Wrong—
Conviction gives him courage and Valor makes him
    strong;
On to'rds Truth's goal he battles, clear Duty's call he
    heeds,
Love binds him to his fellows, a Brother's right he
    pleads;
No creeds nor color blinds him in Nation's direst needs!

FUNERAL HYMN

Phœbe A. Hanaford

(Air: "Mount Vernon")

HUSHED to-day are the sounds of gladness,
    From the mountains to the sea;
And the plaintive voice of sadness
    Rises, mighty God, to Thee.

Freedom claimed another martyr;
    Heaven received another saint:
Who are we, Thy will to question?
    Lord, we weep without complaint.

May we, to Thy wisdom bowing,
    Own Thy love in this dark spell,
While with tears a mighty nation
    Buries one it loved so well!

And, O Thou who took our leader,
    With the Promised Land in view,
While on Pisgah's height we leave him,
    Lead us, Lord, the Jordan through.

LET THERE BE LIGHT

John Pierpont

FROM the beginning the Eternal Cause
Hath wrought according to eternal laws—
Laws on Himself imposed; and His almight
Gives and obeys His law—"Let there be light!"
His great antagonist, the Evil One,
Says, as *his* first command, "Put out the sun!"
As poor Othello, jealous of his wife,
Loving, yet goaded on to take her life,
Steals in, his hand upon his dagger's handle—
But finds himself unable while the candle
Its beautifying beams upon her throws,
Showing such loveliness in such repose,
Steps back, o'erpowered, as would most other men—
And, shaking, says, "Put out the light," and then—
"I can not kill her when I see my mark;
But I can do it if the room is dark!"
So is it with all servants of the devil:
They shun the light because their deeds are evil.
'Twas thus with Booth. The murderer came by
        night,
Skulked up unseen, though all around was light,
And, when the deed was done—the warm blood
        spilt—
Plunged into darkness, friendly to his guilt.
Thus has it been since man first slew his brother:
Darkness and wrong have courted one another.
The courtship ends in wedlock; then begins
The large and fertile family of sins.
The lazy loafer, when naught else is left,
Must "stay his stomach upon fraud or theft;"
The swindler will, of course, the fraud deny;
And every theft is pregnant with a lie;

211

Then lie kills lie, whene'er they meet abroad,
And fraud expires, stabbed by a sharper fraud.
The burglar cuts his brother burglar's throat,
And picks his pocket of a spurious note,
Which he palms off to pay a gambling bet,
Or bilks his butcher of an honest debt.

To such expedients knaves resort, to shirk
God's first commandment—"Thou, to live, must
    work."
Thanks for God's word to Adam when He said,
"Thou with a sweating face shalt eat thy bread."
Many there are who deem this word a curse,
Thinking, than labor there is nothing worse,
A blessed curse, if curse we can it call,
That in this sentence followed "Adam's fall."
Yet man, shortsighted man, has madly striven
To avert this blessing of benignant Heaven,
Has sought the pleasures and the power of wealth,
By crafty artifice, by fraud, by stealth,
To get his bread by some ingenious plan
Or by the sweating face of some more honest man.

The stronger savage aye his task will shirk,
And make the weaker woman do his work.
The conquering soldier came, in time, to yield
Part of his trophies of the battle-field;
Money, not mercy, prompted him to save
His captive's life, and *sell him as a slave!*
Hence feuds were fanned to flame, and wars were
    waged,
Hosts rushed to conflict and the battle raged,
Not that each chief his foeman's blood might spill;
His aim to capture rather than to kill.
The victor spared the foe he might have slain,
Tied him with thongs or bound him with a chain,

And kept him toiling in his field or fold,
Or to another gave him up for gold.
Thus slavery came, by God and man abhorred,
Its ugly parents—avarice and the sword;
Its only office, that hard work he shun,
Whereby all glory, all true wealth are won.
To real greatness man is never *born,*
Nor yet to idle hands fill Plenty's horn.
The leaky craft, just on destruction's brink,
Says to the seaman, "Work your pump or sink!"
The frozen field, beneath whose surface lie
Undug potatoes, says, "Root hog, or die!"
And the first law by God imposed on man
Which, we have seen, in Paradise began,
Imposed to shield the race from want and vice,
And which obeyed makes earth a paradise,
Is clearly stated by the Apostle Paul,
In terms that must be understood by all;
And which, in one line, we will here repeat:
"Who will not labor, neither let him eat."
Slavery, reversing this divine command,
Lifts to insulting heaven her lily hand,
Waving her sword or brandishing her dirk,
And swears that *she* will neither starve *nor* work;
And hence has striven this ordinance to fix,
For all the last four thousand of the six
Of our bright planet's periods round the sun,
Since man on earth his race began to run,
Namely: "Regardless of the right or wrong,
The weak shall labor to support the strong.
Who labors not shall live on finest wheat,
Who labors not shall feed on fattest meat;
Who fats and kills the ox, his bones may gnaw;
Who sows and reaps the wheat, may eat the straw;
The idlest hands shall stuff the busiest jaws;
These are my fixed, my fundamental laws."

THE PRAISE OF LINCOLN

What is the good wherewith this code is fraught?
What are the blessings slavery hath brought?
Ay, where, in the wide field that she has trod,
And o'er it plied her shackles and her rod,
Hath not this fiend left traces of her hand,
Diffused her blight, and pressed her burning brand?
Where hath she brought a single blessing? Where
A sweeter flower, or a more balmy air?
More richly robed the earth in golden corn;
Sung holier hymns to Heaven at even or morn,
Or with more fruits filled Amalthea's horn?

Ancient Dominion, where the bondman's tread,
First on our shores was felt, lift up thy head!
Thy loving arms were first around him thrown,
In thine embrace he loosed thy virgin zone,
Closest and longest to thy bosom pressed,
Thou'st held the laboring bondman to thy breast,
Lift up thy head—once proud,—and show thy race
What are the fruits of that long, close embrace!
What did the bondman find thee when ye met?
What hath he left—he hath not left thee yet!
He found thee fairest of the sister train;
Thy broad deep rivers rolling to the main;
From the wood-crowned Blue Ridges that divide
Ohio's waters from the ocean tide;
Thy valleys, fertile as the fields that smile,
In green and gold, along the ancient Nile.
Thy hillsides, dark with naval oaks and pines,
And teeming with their coal and iron mines;
Thy waterfalls, echoing among the hills,
And clamorous for employment on thy mills,
That from the thundering car and groaning wain,
Would take thy sacks, bursting with golden grain,
And, with their arms unwearied, fill with bread
Each lordly mansion and each humble shed;

That its blue wreath of smoke would ever send
Up to the genial skies, that o'er thee bend;
While, in thy inland sea, their sails unfurled,
Might ride secure the navies of the world.
Such was thy beauty, such thy noble dower,
Couched, as a queen, beneath thy leafy bower,
In thy rich robes of flowers and foliage dressed,
By balmy breezes lovingly caressed
Thou fairest, richest, proudest of the States,
When, to the slave, thou openedst first thy gates.

What hath been wrought upon thee by his hand?
Thy wasted forests, thine exhausted land,
Thy fields unfenced, thy cattle few and lean,
Thine ancient mansions fall'n, thy new ones mean,
Thy broad-leaved poisonous plant that shades thy
        soil,
And makes the laborer languish at his toil,
The withering flowers that deck thy faded face,
Lazy unthrift, and labor in disgrace,
These show the world,—and they may read who
        run—
The work that thy blind slaves, and lords more blind
        have done.

Ancient Dominion, have I done thee wrong?
Say'st thou my colors are laid on too strong?
Then I will gladly lay my pencil down,
And trust thou wilt not blast me with thy frown
If I exhibit of thy blighted land,
Thy portrait painted by a friendly hand.
The great Missourian's picture thou shalt see;
Thou knew'st him well, and well did he know thee.

Missouri's Senator, well known to Fame,
Whom some "the Old Roman," some "Old Bullion"
        name,

215

THE PRAISE OF LINCOLN

Thus paints thy land along Potomac's side,
Near where Virginia's and the Nation's pride,
Thrice honored lived, and long lamented, died.

"Throughout this region, long by slavery curst,
Behold man's progress upon earth reversed.
Backwards and downwards everything goes on:
Houses dilapidated, tenants gone.
Where once were crowds there now is ample room;
Fields fertile once, are now grown up with broom.
No crops, no fences now the plain adorn;
Grass and pine saplings take the place of corn.
As men grow scarce, wild beasts more frequent
        prowl,
The fox grows bolder, oftener hoots the owl,
And hungry wolves are heard more savagely to howl.
The tenant's lot, who here puts in his seed,
Is hopeless, is deplorable indeed;
In vain does he solicit, day by day,
Gravel and grit and still more heartless clay.
The corn and oats that man and horse demand,
He brings not from these fields of pine and sand.
Not long ago, I passed this region o'er,
My journey lay along Potomac's shore,
As the broad-bosomed river gently sweeps
Near where the Father of his Country sleeps.
Riding along the rough highway, and thinking,
I know not what—as Horace says—a clinking
I heard among the stones, on the hillside,
I checked my horse, and looking up, espied
Some negro laborers hoeing with their hoes,
Digging small holes, in equidistant rows,
And burying something in them. So I cried,
'What are you doing there?' A slave replied—
'We're planting corn, sir, in these gravel beds.'
'What plant ye with it?' Answer, 'Herring-heads.'

'Why plant ye herring-heads with corn?' said I.
'To make the corn come up,' was the reply.
Again I asked, 'How many heads do you
Plant, to each grain of corn?' He answered, 'Two.'
'Well, how high grows it, thus manured, I beg?'
'About so high,' measuring upon his leg."
Mother of Presidents, once haughty land,
Behold thy portrait by a master's hand!

One artist more depicts thy state forlorn,
Native is he, and "to the manner born."
His handiwork may fascinate thine eyes;
High-born is he, and *nominally* Wise.
Stumping the State its highest chair to gain,
And, history tells us, stumping not in vain;
This limner, true to nature, thus bewails
His mother's fate: "Commerce her fickle sails
Long since has spread and sailed from you away;
Plowing no more the bosom of your bay;
Your coal mines, richer than are mines of gold,
Remain undug, till your own hearths are cold.
Your iron foundries wait impatient for
Trip-hammer, such as Vulcan wields, or Thor.
Nor of your coarsest cotton, do you spin
Enough to hide your negroes' naked skin.
Of commerce, manufactures, arts, bereft,
Nought but the culture of your ground is left.
And such a culture! He that owns the fee
Leases his land, and skins the poor lessee;
The poor lessee, by his unskilful toil,
Takes his revenge, and skins, in turn, the soil.
Instead of farms, where each his acres tills,
Then cattle feeding upon clovered hills,
We see the landlord's hireling overseer,
His hunger whetted to its keenest edge,

For a tough steak chasing his stump-tailed steer,
Through swamps undrained, and patches rank with
    sedge."
Such was Virginia, stripped of all disguises,
As painted by the *wisest of her Wises*.

To that low point had slavery brought down
Proud old Virginia ere she hanged John Brown:
And the same course, that wrought Virginia's fall,
Was, like the cholera, sweeping over all,
That sat in darkness, on the plains that spread
'Twixt Rio Grande's and Potomac's bed,
Where Abel tilled the ground and Cain ate up the
    bread.
Brown saw Virginia as she, languid stood,
In her slave shambles selling her own blood,
And would have freed her laborer from his chains,
And clothed with verdure her old naked plains;
But she would still on her destroyer dote,
And hug the vampire closer to her throat,
Till, as her pulses faint and fainter throb,
Finding that she must either die or rob,
She bargains with her sisters, who combine,
Such as fair Flora and warm Caroline,
To lay their hands on all that they can get
To eat at leisure and not pay the sweat.

The boldest backwoods hunter justly fears
The hungry wolf he holds but by the ears;
Seeing his hold's so weak, the brute's so strong,
That, without help, he can not hold him long,
And fearing that, if he lets go, his grim
And wide-mouthed game will soon make game of
    him,
Calls on his fellow-huntsmen for their help,
In keeping down and mastering the whelp;

And if his neighbors come not at his call,
He grows profane, and swears he'll whip them all;
So our man-hunters, grappling with a foe,
They scarce can hold, and dare not let him go,
Call, in their terror, upon Northern smiths
And woodmen, for new fetters and green withes,
To bind their shaggy Samson in his mill,
To help them hold, and keep him grinding still,
Nor *him* alone, his children must they bind,
Build them more mills wherein his boys must grind,
Purchase new acres at their proper cost,
Get new Virginias for them to exhaust;
Throw up new dikes 'gainst Freedom's overflow,
And to her surges say, "No farther go!"
And now, forsooth, because those neighbors stand,
Look calmly on, and lend no helping hand,
To their demand for aid, make no reply,
Or coolly say, "We've our own fish to fry;
Good friends, we're weary of this thankless task,
We've given you more than you've a right to ask;
Till now, we've helped you in your time of need,
Conceded till we can no more concede,
Done for you all that should or *will* be done,
So hold your wolf yourself, or—let him run"—
Our Nimrods—mighty hunters—grow profane,
Break *three* commandments, *take God's name in vain,*
Steal from their neighbors, till they've stolen their
    fill,
And then, proceed to bully and to *kill.*

And that is War! But War, that burns and blights,
God makes his minister, and clothes with rights:
The right a bondman's fetters to unclasp,
To wrest the scepter from a rebel's grasp,
And say, "Lay down your cowskin and your dirk,
And take your choice, sir, *starve, or go to work!*"

THE PRAISE OF LINCOLN

This said the man, raised up and sent, through grace,
To be "a prince and savior" of a race;

A race long doomed to servitude and scorn;
But through this Prince's word, to freedom born.
The man to whom the bloody hand of War
Brought the Commission, so long waited for,
"Deliverance to the captives" to proclaim,
Like him whose name "is above every name."
For him a Nation's eyes with tears are dim:
He slavery slew, then slavery murdered him.
But in a race redeemed he made his mark
On History's page. But that race, O how dark—
When darkness covered all the cloud-wrapt land,
And the Oppressor laid his heaviest hand,
Upon its eye-balls, to "put out the light"
Of hope and science from both soul and sight—
Must it be now, when from his "long despair,"
Brought out to feel the sun, and breathe the upper
            air!

Father of lights! for these, thy children long
Held in the dark by robbery and wrong,
Held, groping on in more than Egypt's night,
Hear we not now Thy word "Let there be light?"
For them didst Thou a great Deliverer raise,
For him we all now offer Thee our praise;
And, that his name may never be forgot,
Would his redeemed ones, near the holy spot,
Where his great word went forth, and where he fell,
Build up a monument, the world to tell,
The gratitude of all, who now are free,
Should feel, and *do* feel both to him and Thee.
Not such a monument as Egypt's kings
Built for their bones; but such a one as brings

THE PRAISE OF LINCOLN

Out from the hidings of oblivion's veil,
The hallowed name of Harvard and of Yale,
Within whose shadow, thirsty youths, who think,
With Solomon, that "light is sweet," may drink
From the sweet fountain Thou hast made o'erflow
From all Thy works, above, around, below,
Fountain of *Knowledge,* that, like thine own grace,
Debars no color, and excludes no race,
Where every child may see that, every hour
He's gaining knowledge, he is gaining power;
The power to labor for the common weal;
To soothe some grief, some malady to heal;
And, by example to make all men see,
That it is best for all, that all men should be free.

Our Lincoln Monument of One shall speak,
Like Moses faithful, and like Moses meek;
Who led Thy people through a redder sea
Than Israel passed, to light and liberty.
Of him who humbly trusting in the Lord,
Moved by the Holy Spirit, spake Thy word;
And, as that word was plainly, *firmly* spoken,
The bondman's chains fell off, the tyrant's rod was
       broken.

ABRAHAM LINCOLN

Frank B. Sanborn

THOUGH forts are stormed and cities won,
   And banded Treason melts away,
As sullen mists that hate the sun
   Flee at the bright assault of Day—
   Our heavy hearts will not be gay.

THE PRAISE OF LINCOLN

For thee we mourn, in victory's hour,
  Whose courage no defeat could shake;
Who held'st the State's resistless power
  In trust but for thy people's sake:
  For thee thy people mourning make.

For He that sways the world with love
  (Though War and Wrath His angels are)
Throned thee all earthly kings above,
  On threatened Freedom's flaming car,
  To frighten tyrants, near and far.

His purpose high thy course impelled
  O'er War's red height and smoldering plain;
When awe, when pity thee withheld,
  He gave thy chafing steeds the rein,
  Till at thy feet lay Slavery slain.

Then ceased thy task—another hand
  Takes up the burden thou lay'st down;
Sorrowing and glad, the rescued land
  Twofold awards thy just renown—
  The Victor's and the Martyr's crown.

HYMN

Jones Very

(Sung at the Eulogy of Abraham Lincoln, June 1st, 1865)

O GOD! who dost the nations lead,
  Though oft in ways to them unknown,
We look to Thee in this our need;
  A supplicant people seek Thy throne.

THE PRAISE OF LINCOLN

For he whom Thou didst raise to guide
   Has fallen by the assassin's hand;
In Thee alone would we confide
   To guide, to guard, to save our land.

Through perils great, from year to year,
   Thou hast thus far our nation brought,
And given the victory to cheer,
   And by our Chief deliverance wrought.

With earnest prayer he sought Thy will
   In all the great events of life;
And nobly did his work fulfill,
   Through four long years of bloody strife.

Oh, lift us up in this sad hour,
   Let not our Country's foes prevail;
Sustain us by Thy mighty power,
   Let not to us Thy promise fail.

May Justice, Liberty, and Peace,
   For which his life he freely gave,
Bless all our land, and never cease
   To shed their glory round his grave.

THE FUNERAL DIRGE

L. M. Dawn

ALL our land is draped in mourning,
Hearts are bowed and strong men weep;
For our loved, our noble leader,
Sleeps his last, his dreamless sleep—
Gone forever is our hero,
Fallen by a traitor's hand,
Though preserved his dearest treasure,
Our redeem'd, beloved land.
     Rest in peace.

Through our night of bloody struggle,
Ever dauntless, firm and true,
Bravely, gently forth he led us,
Till the morn burst on our view—
Till he saw the day of triumph,
Saw the field our heroes won,
Then his honored life was ended,
Then his glorious work was done.
   Rest in peace.

When from mountain, hill and valley,
To their homes our brave boys come,
When with welcome notes we greet them,
Song and cheer and pealing drum,
When we miss our loved ones fallen,
When to weep we turn aside,
Then for him our tears shall mingle—
He has suffered, he has died.
   Rest in peace.

Honored leader, long and fondly
Shall thy memory cherished be,
Hearts shall bless thee for their freedom,
Hearts unborn shall sigh for thee.
He who gave thee might and wisdom
Gave thy spirit sweet repose,
Farewell, guardian, friend, and father,
Rest forever, rest in peace.
   Rest in peace.

HYMN

Abner Cheney Goodell, Jr.

O Thou who givest life
 And takest it again;
Who, as a Father lovingly,
 O'er all mankind dost reign;

224

THE PRAISE OF LINCOLN

Our refuge and protector when
  The King of kings was slain,—

In this our time of grief
  And doubt we come to Thee!
Thou only canst assuage our grief;
  And, from Thy throne, we see
That, in the things we chiefly doubt
  There is no mystery.

If we did never turn
  Away from Thy dear face,
If we did never faithless grow
  And loosen Thy embrace,
Then doubt and fear would never find
  In us a dwelling place.

Then, through the deepest gloom
  That ever shrouds our way,
Our hearts would never faint,—our eyes
  Would never miss the ray
Which, like the rising morning-star,
  Heralds the perfect day.

Trusting Thy sovereign will,
  Confiding in Thy care,—
As knowing that Thou kinder art
  Than earthly parents are,
And that thou lovest whom Thou call'st
  The cruel cross to bear,—

Then we should cease to mourn
  For them—the good and wise—
Whom Thou dost set on earth to be
  A light unto our eyes,
But whom, in Thy good time, Thou tak'st
  To be in Paradise.

THE FUNERAL HYMN

Phineas Densmore Gurley

REST, noble martyr! rest in peace;
    Rest with the true and brave,
Who, like thee, fell in Freedom's cause,
    The Nation's life to save.

Thy name shall live while time endures,
    And men shall say of thee,
"He saved the country from its foes,
    And bade the slave be free."

These deeds shall be thy monument,
    Better than brass or stone;
They leave thy fame in glory's light,
    Unrivaled and alone.

This consecrated spot shall be
    To Freedom ever dear;
And Freedom's sons of every race
    Shall weep and worship here.

O God! before whom we, in tears,
    Our fallen chief deplore,
Grant that the cause, for which he died,
    May *live* for evermore.

Doxology:

To Father, Son, and Holy Ghost,
    The God whom we adore,
Be glory as it was, is now,
    And shall be evermore.

226

NOTES

Page 1. By many people this is thought to be Whitman's best poem. It was written in 1865, soon after the occurrence of the tragedy. In this poem he forsakes his peculiar style, which many admire and many more abominate, and falls either consciously or unconsciously into rhythm and meter. Mr. Whitman and Mr. Lincoln were personal friends, and there is perhaps no other poem of similar length in the language, containing so much of pathos and genuine feeling.

Page 5. We give here merely that part of Lowell's *Ode Recited at the Harvard Commemoration,* which refers to the life and character of Lincoln. The lines on Lincoln were not included in the poem as the poet gave it at the Commemoration exercises, but they were added immediately afterward. The part of the Ode here given is the part that is most highly prized.

Page 8. These stanzas were read by the late Julia Ward Howe, at exercises held in Boston commemorating the hundredth anniversary of Lincoln's birth.

Page 20. The author of these stanzas is supposedly English. The poem first appeared in the pages of *Macmillan's Magazine,* London.

Page 34. One of the most remarkable tributes to Lincoln that came from the press was from the London *Punch* which, by word and picture, had ridiculed him without mercy. The author, singularly enough, was also author of *Our American Cousin,* the play the president was attending when shot. The poem was published May 6, 1865.

Page 41. This poem by Leland was first published in the *Continental Magazine.* It is said to be the first poem written on the Proclamation of Emancipation issued by President Lincoln, September 22, 1862, and proclaimed to be in effect January 1, 1863.

Page 51. Merely that part of Taylor's *Gettysburg Ode* relating to Lincoln, is given.

Page 52. The Lincoln Boulder is an immense boulder taken from the Hudson River, and placed upon the library grounds of Nyack, New York, by the soldiers and citizens of that city, as a memorial to Abraham Lincoln. The face of the boulder contains a bronze tablet with Lincoln's Gettysburg Address. The dedicatory exercises were held June 13, 1908.

Page 53. This poem was written when the author was only twelve years old. He lives at Richmond, Va.

Page 57. For many years the grave of President Lincoln's mother, Nancy Hanks Lincoln, was neglected. About the close of the war a young man named Corbin, from Ohio, who was visiting in the vicinity of Lincoln City, Indiana, made a trip to the grave and wrote a poem on its neglected condition. It was published at the time in a Rockport (Indiana) newspaper over the *nom de plume* "Babbie." Not until a few years ago, long after the author's death, was his name disclosed. In recent years a plot of sixteen acres surrounding the grave was bought by the state, and made into a park, a monument has been built, and the grounds are kept in attractive condition at the state's expense.

Page 59. Frances E. Willard, the distinguished temperance evangelist, while on a tour of the Pacific states, was for a short time a guest in the home of Mr. Alfred H. Nelson, of Ogden, Utah. Miss Willard's host incidentally repeated in her presence part of a poem about Lincoln, which he regarded as the finest ever written on that great theme. Miss Willard expressed her admiration of it, and Mr. Nelson voluntarily furnished her a complete copy written from memory. Mr. Nelson was in Virginia City, Nevada, when Abraham Lincoln's funeral services were celebrated there. He heard the author, who was then editor of the *Territorial Enterprise,* read the poem, and observed the profound impression it produced. The poem was again printed in the *Illinois State Journal,* September 26, 1883.

Pages 72 and 157. These poems by Lyman Whitney Allen are excerpts from the revised edition of the prize poem, *Abraham Lincoln,* published in the New York *Herald,* December 15, 1895.

Page 77. President Lincoln was a firm believer in the significance of dreams. To dream of a ship presaged the coming of some important event. Such dreams came to him before the battles of Antietam, Murfreesboro, Vicksburg and Gettysburg. To him they indicated victory. It seems that on the night of April 13, 1865, he dreamed of seeing "A flying bark with all her canvas bent." He was in doubt as to what this foreshadowed, as the war was practically over.

Page 83. It is said that Mr. Lincoln had an earnest desire to visit the Holy Land, and that just before he was shot he had discussed the matter with Mrs. Lincoln. He told her that when the cares of state were over they would go to Palestine, adding: "There is no city I desire so much to see as Jerusalem."

Page 90. This poem was read before the Tom Reed Republican Club, of Ogden, Utah, on the anniversary of Lincoln's birthday, February 12, 1888. It was pub-

NOTES

lished in *The Poets of Maine,* a volume compiled by
George Bancroft Griffith, and now out of print.

Page 170. Savannah surrendered on the 21st of December, 1864, to General Sherman, who, on the 22nd,
sent a despatch to President Lincoln, presenting to him
"as a Christmas gift, the city of Savannah with one
hundred and fifty heavy guns and plenty of ammuni-
tion, and also about twenty-five thousand bales of
cotton." On December 26th the president replied to
General Sherman: "Many, many thanks for your
Christmas gift, the capture of Savannah . . . it
is indeed a great success."

Page 174. From the Ode delivered before the
Brooklyn Institute of Arts and Sciences at the Acad-
emy of Music, Brooklyn, New York, February, 1909.

Page 183. This memorial poem was written at
Springfield, Illinois, on the twentieth anniversary of
the death of President Lincoln, April 15, 1885.

Page 196. This poem was first published in *Collier's
Weekly,* February, 1909. It was later included in Mr.
Oppenheim's *Monday Morning and Other Poems.*

Page 211. This poem was read by the venerable
New England poet, John Pierpont, on the occasion of
the celebration of the Colored People's Educational
Monument Association in memory of Abraham Lincoln, on the Fourth of July, 1865, in the presidential
grounds, Washington, D. C.

Page 223. This *Funeral Dirge* was set to music by
George F. Root, and sung at the funeral services of
Abraham Lincoln at Washington, D. C.

A. D. W.

INDEXES

OF AUTHORS, TITLES AND FIRST LINES

INDEX OF AUTHORS

INDEX OF AUTHORS

INDEX OF AUTHORS

235

INDEX OF TITLES

INDEX OF TITLES

INDEX OF TITLES

INDEX OF FIRST LINES

INDEX OF FIRST LINES

The Life of Abraham Lincoln

By WILLIAM E. BARTON, author of *The Soul of Abraham Lincoln, The Paternity of Abraham Lincoln*, etc.

Two volumes, profusely illustrated. Index. Large 8vo, clothed, boxed.

THE MOST distinctive contribution to Lincoln literature since William Herndon laid down his pen a half century ago.—Horace Green in *N. Y. Times Book Review*.

Proves that Dr. Barton is one of the few really great biographers of all time.—*International Book Review*.

Will stand as a most notable contribution to the knowledge of one of the greatest figures history has produced.—Forrest P. Hull in *Boston Transcript*.

Dr. Barton's original study of so many phases of Lincoln's history makes his work an outstanding authority on the subject. He makes Lincoln more normally human than previous writers, and the history of his presidency is written with more intimate detail than preceding biographers have supplied.—Professor Luther E. Robinson, in *The Saturday Review*.

No one in years has given us the ambitious work to compare with Dr. Barton's delightful and fascinating biography. It is the most satisfying realistic record of the man Lincoln yet written.—Claude G. Bowers, in *New York World*.

The most authoritative life so far written. In addition, it is exceedingly interesting to read—as fascinating as a romantic novel.—Carrol Binder in *Chicago News*.

Destined to remain for many years as the standard life of the martyred President.—W. J. Ghent in *The Outlook*.

Lincoln

An account of His Personal Life, Especially of its Springs of Action as Revealed and Deepened by the Ordeal of War.

By NATHANIEL WRIGHT STEPHENSON Crown 8vo, uncut front and foot, gilt top. Contains three new and previously unpublished chapters. Illustrated with a Lincoln portrait gallery, showing how his appearance changed as his character developed.

THE LINCOLN story will surely live for many hundreds of years and as long as it lives this book should live with it. It has stirred me more deeply than any American book I have read for years. It is a beautiful book, beautifully conceived, felt and written.—Sherwood Anderson in *The Golden Book*.

A strong, scholarly, brilliant book, really superb. One is refreshed by every page, every paragraph. Whoever doubts the power of style, in and of itself, should read Stephenson's *Lincoln*—and he will doubt no longer. Scholar and philosopher, Mr. Stephenson is also artist.—*Albert J. Beveridge in International Book Review*.

For the first time we have an account of Lincoln which points out the evolution of his character. The most satisfactory both from a literary and a historical point of view.—*Allen Johnson, of Yale*.

The best life of Lincoln. As a work of art, an example of how a biography should be written, it deserves unqualified praise.—*New York Tribune*.